EARLY GUNPOWDER ARTILLERY

*c.*1300–1600

EARLY GUNPOWDER ARTILLERY

c.1300–1600

John Norris

The Crowood Press

First published in 2003 by
The Crowood Press Ltd
Ramsbury, Marlborough
Wiltshire SN8 2HR

www.crowood.com

British Library Cataloguing-in-Publication Data
A catalogue record for this book is available from the British Library.

ISBN 1 86126 615 4

Dedication
All written work encroaches on family life and the normal routine by which it functions on a daily basis. When one undertakes the writing of a book of this nature, the amount of time one spends on preparation and research can lead the authorís spouse to question the reason for making a particular visit. And so it is in this case, when my wife has had to stand by in the pouring rain while I looked at what to her was merely a piece of rusting metal. She stood resolutely while I took notes and photographs, and did not complain over greatly. She has had to listen while I talked to various parties, as well as hearing my musing and thoughts. Elizabeth has accompanied me on many such field trips and it is to her that I dedicate this book by way of saying thank you to her for taking those extra all-important notes.

Typeset by Naomi Lunn.

Printed and bound in by Bookcraft, Midsomer Norton.

Contents

1 Introduction

Artillery is the collective name given to a group of weapons which use the explosive force of gunpowder to propel projectiles from a tube over long range by means of chemical energy. These weapons have been present on the battlefield for so long that they are often taken for granted. However, when gunpowder artillery made its first appearance on the battlefield in the early fourteenth century it was to be some time before its full potential was realized. Indeed, it only came to prominence in a slow, gradual manner over a period of years.

The exact origin of gunpowder is not entirely clear and the place where artillery was invented cannot be pinpointed. Evidence indicates that gunpowder was known before its power was harnessed for destructive purposes by using it in connection with metal tubes, which would become known as cannons. It is generally accepted that no single country could ever lay sole claim to the development of gunpowder artillery. It is more likely that a series of disparate ideas and theories eventually culminated in an invention which would forever change the battlefield. Early artillery weapons were not manufactured to any standard design and it was not unknown for a gun founder to cast each weapon as his fancy or experience dictated.

'ARTILLERY'

The term 'artillery' as we know it today may have evolved from one of a number of different forms. One theory is that the word is a combination of *Arcus*, meaning bow, and *Telum*, meaning projectile. Alternatively, the origin of the word may be attributed to the Latin term *Ars Tolendi*, or *Ars* and *Tirare*, meaning the art of catapulting or shooting. A third possibility is that it is derived from the Latin phrase *Ars Telorum*, referring to the art of long-range weapons. In the seventeenth century, the great siege master and fortress builder, Sebastien le Prestre de Vauban, 1633–1707, announced that he believed that he had traced the origin of the term back to an old French word *Artillier*, which meant to either fortify or arm. On the other hand, the German philologist Diez, believed he could trace the origin of the word back to a Provencal word *Artilha*, which had entered the German language as early as 1500.

Whichever explanation one chooses to accept as the origin of the term artillery, it ultimately refers to a means of propelling a projectile towards an enemy over a distance. In this case, the term can also be applied to those ancient machines of war as fielded by the Greeks and Romans such as the *Catapulta* and *Ballista*. Both of these devices used torsion power to propel their missiles, and pre-date gunpowder by many centuries.

During the early course of its history, artillery developed into various designs with some pieces being given specific identifying names. Some of these names were rather fanciful such as 'falcon', 'ribaldequin' and 'robinet'. Other names are familiar to us even today, such as 'howitzer', 'cannon' and 'mortar'. In fact, the term cannon, most often used in the early years, is believed to be derived from either the Latin word *canna*, meaning tube, or the Greek word *kanun*, also meaning tube, which describe perfectly the appearance of the barrel of a piece of artillery.

7

The Charter of Saint George

During the period referred to as the Middle Ages there was great debate as to what weapons constituted artillery. One of the best and earliest definitions was drawn up during the reign of Henry VIII. In 1537 he issued a Charter for the creation of the Guylde of Saint George, in which he charged them with becoming:

> The overseers of the science of artillery … to witt, long bowes, cross bowes and hand gonnes for the better encrease of the defence of our realme.

For over 460 years this Charter has been maintained by the Honorable Artillery Company, which was raised as a regiment of the British Army, and which can trace its origins directly back to the Guylde of Saint George and the same year in which the Charter was issued.

THE DEVELOPMENT OF HAND-HELD WEAPONS

The reference to 'hand gonnes' in the Charter raises a question regarding the point at which artillery and hand-held gunpowder weapons became divided and subsequently evolved to become two distinguishable types of weapon. Again, it is very difficult to state with any great certainty when the exact transition took place, but it can probably be placed sometime in the fourteenth century and at an early stage in the development of gunpowder weapons. References to *gunnis cum telar* (guns with handles) were recorded in the 1350s, thereby marking the emergence of personal weapons.

In 1411 John the Good, Duke of Burgundy, is recorded as having some 4,000 handguns in his armoury. These weapons would have had an effective range of less than 200yd, about the same range as some of the smaller artillery pieces of the day, but the firer would have been considered fortunate if he had hit his intended target. By 1419 the Hussite troops of the Bohemian leader, Jan Ziska, are recorded as using hand-held gunpowder weapons and tubed gunpowder artillery in their continued struggle against the Emperor Sigismund. All of this evidence points to the fact that by the fifteenth century early handguns were being used alongside artillery by trained infantrymen.

THE MORTAR

The mortar has had a chequered history. The basic shape of this weapon is believed to be have been influenced by the design of the grinding mortar as used by chemists. Being short and stubby in appearance, the mortar was one of the easiest pieces of artillery to manufacture. These weapons were made from several different types of metal, including bronze, brass and latten, and because of their simple shape they could be cast in one piece. Although designs in early cannon improved, the basic shape of the mortar remained unaltered. The cannon of the day were used to fire directly at targets, but mortars fired at angles of elevation greater than 45 degrees. These weapons were used to 'lob' projectiles in a high arc over the walls of besieged castles. Later they would be used to fire projectiles termed as 'bombs', which were hollow shells filled with gunpowder and set to explode by means of a rudimentary fuse.

THE INFLUENCE OF ARTILLERY ON WARFARE

It is now more than 650 years since weapons of tubed artillery, which is to say conventional cannons or guns, were first recorded as being used on the battlefield. As seen from the wording of Henry VIII's Charter, the term artillery has been used to include a variety of weapons, including grenades and rockets. The appearance proper of cannons, in a recognizable form, on the battlefield in the fourteenth century, signalled the end of single-handed combat and ushered in a new military code of conduct. The fifteenth-century soldiers of the condottieri, Gian Paolo Vitelli and Prospero Colonna, declared that: 'Wars are won rather by industry and cunning …'. However, it would not be until the seventeenth century that artillery would come to be used with any great effect against enemy troops ranged in the open rather than against a city or castle under siege.

Early siege engines, which relied on counterpoise, torsion or kinetic energy to launch their projectiles, were also called artillery. Indeed there was a point when both gunpowder and stored-energy artillery were used in conjunction. Several chronicles record a short period in history when attacking forces laying siege to either fortifications or walled cities deployed both ancient, stone throwing, artillery and the newly developed weapons which hurled projectiles using the explosive force of gunpowder in order to batter the walls. As the design of this new form of artillery improved, the older styles passed into obsolescence, leaving the path clear for the further development of yet more powerful weapons. However, stone-throwing artillery was still useful in certain situations, particularly when stocks of gunpowder were exhausted and the besiegers wished to continue their battering of the target walls.

The changes that artillery made to the way which wars were fought began as a gradual process, but once the process was begun there was to be no turning back. In the beginning, during their early introduction, gunpowder weapons were not as accurate as a longbow in the hands of a well trained and experienced archer. As the range of the guns increased, one of the major effects of the use of gunpowder artillery was to deepen the battlefield. Its introduction also created the establishment of a so-called 'third arm' within armies, the others being infantry and cavalry. No longer would battles be fought by armies at distances of only a few hundred yards. Instead, artillery would change this distance to thousands of yards and eventually many miles as technological improvements made the art of gunnery a precise science. With the introduction of gunpowder weapons on the battlefield, it became more important than ever before to train troops to a high degree of proficiency in the use of weapons. Thus rather than being fought at close quarters by masses of poorly trained militia, warfare became the province of more regular and better disciplined troops. Some of these new scientifically minded troops were so highly skilled and experienced that they hired out their services as mercenaries to the highest bidder. This applied to all levels of troops, but particularly so to the gunners with their pieces of artillery. Thus it has been argued that the development of artillery was the driving force behind the establishment of standing armies.

THE AIM OF THIS BOOK

The aim of this book is to chart the manufacturing techniques, tactical roles and functions of artillery over a period of history covering more than 250 years. The battles in which it had a decisive effect are also discussed, as is the way in which the role of artillery adapted to move with the ever-changing face of the battlefield. The contributions made by the individuals and groups who are believed to have had a major influence on the development of gunpowder artillery and the way in which it was used are highlighted. The terms used here to describe pieces of artillery will be, in general, those names and spellings which are most readily recognized.

2 The Emergence of Gunpowder Artillery: 1300 to 1400

Even after many centuries and a great deal of research into the subject, it is not possible to state with absolute certainty when or where gunpowder was first used to propel a projectile from a tube. However, we can be certain that, on being presented with demonstrations of the power of gunpowder, there can have been few military leaders in the thirteenth and fourteenth centuries who would have failed to have been impressed with its potential. Once the power of gunpowder had been revealed it was inevitable that bigger and more powerful weapons would be demanded. This development would take many years, but there could be no stopping the natural process of evolution and certainly no going back.

THE ORIGIN OF GUNPOWDER AND GUNPOWDER WEAPONS

It was only with the discovery of gunpowder that development of weapons based on its use could begin. However, there are several different theories regarding the origin of gunpowder. Some historians postulate that the substance may be Arabic in origin, where it could have been discovered as the side effect of early experimentation into alchemy, which aimed to turn base metals, such as lead, into gold. However, strong evidence points towards gunpowder being first discovered in China. This is supported by a number of facts, not the least of which is the existence of an early reference, chronicled *c.* 908AD, which recounts the use of gunpowder by Chinese troops who used the compound to generate noise to unnerve the enemy and to demol-

ish structures. Another early written account mentioning gunpowder is a military treatise by Wu Ching Tsung Yao, believed to have been written around 1044, in which he outlines the formula for combining the three constituent compounds of gunpowder. This is very strong evidence in favour of the theory that gunpowder could have been discovered in China as early as the eighth century, where its properties were accidentally discovered as a result of experiments into producing an elixir of life.

Early Developments in China

Whatever its exact origins, the earliest recorded use of gunpowder to propel a projectile, possibly no more than a ball of clay, from a device which would later become recognizable as a weapon, is given in Chinese chronicles, which describe a long-barrelled bamboo apparatus bound in either leather or rope for additional strength. This very basic, but effective, device is believed to have been developed by the Chinese General Ch'en Gui, the commander of the garrison of Anlu, in the Hopei Province who, it is recounted, used the weapon in about 1132AD. Although crude in concept and lacking refinement, it nevertheless demonstrates that serious thought had been applied to advance the technology which would lead to the developing of larger gunpowder weapons. The reliability factor of this crude device, sometimes referred to as *huo ch'iang*, would have been virtually non-existent and its safety would have been highly questionable. In fact, it may even have been equally as dangerous to the user as the intended target. As regards accuracy, it would be safe to say that such a device would have been of most use in frightening horses and troops who had little or no experience of such a weapon. A further 200 years were to pass from the time of the appearance of General Ch'en Gui's weapon before true gunpowder artillery would emerge, that is to say the point at which weapons with barrels manufactured from metal and capable of discharging projectiles can be said conclusively to have been used by the Chinese in battle.

One of the first accounts of the use of gunpowder artillery in China appears in 1341, when Chang Hsien composed a verse called 'The Iron Cannon Affair', in which he describes the firing of a gunpowder weapon which is referred to as an 'eruptor'. Whether or not he actually witnessed the effects at first hand is unknown, but it is through the written accounts of chroniclers such as Chang Hsien, and his European contemporaries, that the efficacy of these early weapons is recorded. Although basic in design, this early Chinese device was, nevertheless, a deadly weapon which could, in the words of Hsien, 'pierce the heart or belly when it strikes a man or horse, and can even transfix several persons at once'. Even when one allows for technical inaccuracies in the translation, and allegorical or poetic licence on behalf of the writer,

the account is quite vivid and continues:

> The black dragon lobbed over an egg-shaped thing
> Fully the size of a peck measure it was,
> And it burst, and a dragon flew out with peals of thunder rolling
> In the air it was like a blazing and flashing fire.
> The first bang was like the dividing of chaos in two,
> As if the mountains and rivers were all turned upside down

Close examination of this description would lead one to believe that the Chinese were using gunpowder artillery with exploding shells long before the technique was developed in Western Europe. The noted and distinguished historian, Dr Joseph Needham, has concurred with the above description, and also terms early Chinese gunpowder weapons as 'eruptors'. If the event is correctly recorded by Chang Hsien, it indicates that the use of gunpowder artillery may have been well established in China five years before very basic artillery weapons of a similar nature were recorded as being used by the English army at the Battle of Crécy in France.

Gunpowder Comes to Europe

The way in which gunpowder came to the Europe is almost as mysterious as the origins of the actual substance itself. The introduction of gunpowder is clouded by uncertainty, which is compounded by the fact that its history is littered by figures such as the almost fantasy-like figure of Berthold Schwartz, reputedly a monk from Freiburg in Germany. However, it has come to be accepted that stocks of prepared gunpowder probably arrived in Europe via the Middle East, along the trade routes from China. These trade routes are known to have existed from before the time of Marco Polo, whose family traded out of Italy in the thirteenth and fourteenth centuries. It was along these well-established routes that traders, such as the Arabs, are believed to have brought with them not only the secret of how to manufacture gunpowder but

also how to use it to propel stone or metal projectiles from metal tubes specially made for that purpose.

A second theory is that gunpowder was brought to eastern Europe during the Mongol invasion in the first half of the thirteenth century. Indeed it is quite possible that the Mongols could have brought it with them, during their attacks into Europe in 1241–1242, because they are known to have used gunpowder and other specific types of incendiary devices fitted with simple fuses which were lit just before being used. These devices were given names such as *chen t'ien lei* (thunder bomb) and were used to produce noise in order to cause confusion among their enemies. These devices had undoubtedly been acquired, in turn, during the Mongol conquest of China, where they had been in use for some considerable period of time.

Gunpowder Comes to Europe *continued*

With the death of Ogedai Khan, in 1242, the western advance by the Mongols came to an abrupt halt when their armies were recalled to elect a new Khan. In the haste of their departure, it is quite possible that they may have left behind some discarded gunpowder-based devices such as the *tu-yao yen ch'iu* (poison and smoke ball). This device is known to have contained sulfur, nitre, aconite (a poisonous plant related to the wolfsbane family), oil, charcoal, resin and wax. Truly it was a deadly combination and one which included all of the constituent ingredients for gunpowder. This spherical, hollow receptacle was made from clay and weighed about 2kg, light enough to permit it to be either hand-thrown, in the manner of an early hand grenade, or launched from a catapult siege engine using torsion energy. According to the writings of Miu Yu-Sun, who in turn quotes Yu Wei, a minor scholar, states that in the second half of the thirteenth century a Mongol by the name of Ch'i Wu Wen travelled into Europe taking with him the complete working knowledge of gunpowder and gunnery technology of the time.

If this second theory is held to be correct, this would provide an explanation for the basis of the writings of Roger Bacon and Albertus Magnus. It is mainly through the writings of Bacon, however, that we have come to understand the workings and composition of early gunpowder recipes. Indeed, there is much credit to believe that Roger Bacon, *c.* 1214–1294, an English Fransican monk of Ilchester, was one of the first people in Europe to understand the power of the newly discovered fiery and explosive properties of gunpowder, or black powder as it was termed at the time. Albertus Magnus, 1200–1280, a Dominican Friar, later to be beatified in 1622 and finally made a saint by Pope Pius XI in 1931, was born to a noble military family in Bavaria and well educated in the natural sciences. As such his name is also attached to a small, indeed select, number of Europeans who knew of gunpowder. However, of these two figures it was Bacon, in 1242, who, at the age of about twenty-eight years, wrote down the facts surrounding his findings into the effects of gunpowder in his work entitled *Epistolae de Secretis Operibus Artus et Naturae et de Nullitate Magiae*.

In a move which has come to be regarded as Bacon's means of protecting the secret of gunpowder, he wrote of it in the form of a cryptogram. For example he referred to saltpeter and sulfur as *Luru mone cap ubre* and powdered charcoal was written as *car-bonum pulvere*. Using his own secret code, which has now been deciphered, Bacon wrote of his findings and recorded how a portion of this powder when wrapped in parchment could be lit by a flame to cause an explosion coupled with a loud report. This would conform with the widely held theory that he, in turn, could have learned of the existence of gunpowder through stories recounting this new substance left in the wake of the Mongols' retreat in the same year.

Bacon describes the method of manufacturing the powder to produce 'thunder and lightning' and how the ingredients were to be mixed on a slab of marble, then the powder to be wrapped in parchment and ignited to produce a 'blinding flash and stunning noise'. Bacon gave the proportions for mixing gunpowder, which has been interpreted as being 7:5:5 saltpeter, charcoal and sulfur. In a translation of part of his works on the subject he is shown to have written:

> This powder is enclosed in an instrument of parchment the size of a finger, and since this can make a noise which seriously distresses the ears of men, especially if one is taken unawares, and the terrible flash is also very alarming, if an instrument of large size were used, no one could stand the terror of the noise and flash. If the instrument were made of solid material the violence would be much greater.

While he did not invent cannons or firearms, Bacon had recognized the power of the compound with which he was experimenting and left suggestions for following generations.

It is ironic that at the time of these discoveries by such ecclesiastical figures, the Church was expressing its detestation of anyone who manufactured fiery substances for war-like purposes. This sense of anathema towards incendiary materials extended to Greek Fire, an early type of napalm which was still in limited use, and naturally included gunpowder. The Church was vehement in its hatred of any form of firearm and decried the use of such, to the point of declaring that anyone using them was guilty of committing blasphemy by dabbling in the Black Arts. Despite this ruling from such a powerful body, gunpowder weapons continued to be developed and their usage spread. In fact by the mid-fourteenth century the army of the Pope would also be equipped with artillery and gunpowder weapons. Early written works on artillery instructed men involved with 'such

Gunpowder Comes to Europe *continued*

devilish instruments of destruction, never to forget their Christian responsibilities and to always have the vision of God before their eyes'.

At this time gunpowder was termed 'black powder' because of its black colour, which was a result of the large percentage of charcoal in its composition. Another, rather inexplicable, name for this volatile compound was 'serpentine', believed by some to derive from the fact that its granular appearance resembled the scale-like texture of a snake's skin. The full danger of this powder was still largely misunderstood, and some homilies soon built up, such as the one which considered it 'unseemly' for gunners to stand on any gunpowder which had been spilled on the ground. The reason behind this was not simply due to some battlefield military etiquette, but to avoid accidental combustion due to the friction of leather-soled boots, especially if the action was performed on a rough and hard stony surface.

In his later essays, *c.*1260, Roger Bacon began to refer more openly to the existence of gunpowder, when he writes of 'the powder, known in divers places, composed of saltpeter, sulfur and charcoal'. Several years after the death of Bacon, a series of written works attributed to the rather strange figure known as Marcus Graecus (Mark the Greek), *c.* 1300, appeared and he is credited as being the author of a compiled collection of works in a volume entitled *Book of Fires for the Burning of Enemies.* Apart from only one original formula for gunpowder, given as 6:1:2 parts saltpeter, sulfur and charcoal, the work simply a compendium reiterating some of the earlier writings on the subject, including the formula, in cryptograph form, given by Roger Bacon. The figure of Marcus Graecus is now believed to be a nom de plume used by someone who may have been either a Byzantine Greek or an Arab converted to Western ideals and Chritianity, and therefore wished to remain anonymous. By *c.* 1400 the artillerist Montauban would give his ideal proportions for mixing black powder as 22:4:5 parts per ingredient. As might be expected, there was no standardized rate of mixing black powder and it is possible that the mixture varied from one country to another and even from one centre of production to another.

On ignition, a given weight of black powder will produce a large volume of gas, which in the confined space of a barrel rapidly expands and builds up to produce considerable pressure. Such expanding gases naturally vent through the easiest point of exit, which in the case of a gun barrel is the open end or muzzle, with some 90 per cent of the pressure being exerted towards the thickened breech end of the barrel. This venting gas moves very quickly and in turn will exert pressure on an object which is fitted into the barrel, causing it to move forward at velocity. This phenomenon, if not the exact mathematics, must have been realized by the early gunners, and would explain why cannons of the thirteenth century had very thick walls to the sides of the barrels. However, the measurements of loading an accurate charge of black powder into a gun would remain ambiguous for some time and was left to the judgement of the individual gunner. Black powder was expensive to manufacture and it has been calculated that in England around the year 1346 that it cost some 18 pence to produce one pound of the substance; the equivalent to almost £90 per kilo at present-day prices. By 1376, the demand for gunpowder had risen sharply, and the price for a kilo of gunpowder had increased nine-fold to £1.20. This was due to a number of factors such as labour costs, along with the costs of gathering and transportation of the constituent compounds. It should be remembered that at this time the weekly wage for a manual labourer was paid in only pennies and that fortifications, such as the brick-built Caister Castle, near Yarmouth in Norfolk, built between 1432 and 1435, was erected for the sum of only £1,480. The high cost of producing gunpowder was offset by the results that early cannon yielded on the battlefield, by spreading confusion and panic among an enemy whose troops had never before encountered such weapons. Furthermore, castles and large cities under siege could be forced into submission with the minimum expenditure in effort and manpower.

A monk called Berthold Schwartz is often credited with discovering the propellant properties of black powder by igniting the compound in a vessel to discharge an object. There exists an engraving, tentatively dated at 1380, which purportedly shows the reactions of Black Berthold (which is a general translation of his German name) at the moment of discovery. If this is to be taken as the date for which the foundations of artillery were laid, it would throw the generally accepted chronological development of the history of artillery on its head. Some references state that the experiment took place in 1320, and that Berthold Schwartz was injured during the incident, when his apothecary's grinding mortar exploded as he was reducing the mixture for gunpowder. The

Gunpowder Comes to Europe *continued*

story is apocryphal and continues in the same vein, sometimes with conjectural conversation, to relate how the incident gave rise to the expression of the term 'mortar' as an artillery piece.

However, there are a number of anomalies concerning the actual existence of this mysterious figure. Firstly, there is no conclusive or historical evidence to support the fact that Berthold Schwartz ever truly existed apart from in the fervid mind of the engraver. Brigadier O.F.G. Hogg concurs with other historians, such as J.R. Hartington, and dismisses the figure of Schwartz as an 'anthropomorphic mirage of history'. Furthermore, the term 'mortar' as a form of artillery was not to be coined until many years after the supposed incident in Schwartz's workshop. The theory that this monk did not, in fact, exist is further borne out by the fact, that unlike Bacon and Albertus Magnus, Schwartz left no written work covering his findings.

The fact remains that the first European battle in which gunpowder artillery is reliably recorded as being used was the Battle of Crécy, where English troops under Edward III deployed between three and five cannons, in August 1346. These devices are referred to as either *roundelades* or *pots de fer*, the latter name appears to be the more popular and widespread name to the point where it is commonly used to refer to early cannon. Although an exact translation would give us 'pots of iron', another term, *pots de*

feu, was also in usage at the time. The first significant European battlefield deployment of gunpowder weapons pre-dates the 1380 engraving of Schwartz's supposed experiments by thirty-four years and even earlier records pre-date his experiments by almost sixty years. Furthermore, the composition of gunpowder from the time was recorded by John Ardenne, a surgeon during the reign of Edward III, who wrote that it contained:

> 12 pounds of live sulpher, 2 pounds of willow charcoal, 6 pounds of saltpeter, if they be well ground on a slab of marble, then sift the powder through a fine kerchief … This powder is useful for throwing balls of iron or lead or brass from an instrument they call a Gonne.

Despite the fact that such evidence is well recorded and completely dispels the theory that, if he existed, Schwartz mastered the use of gunpowder as a propellant for artillery, many histories still make reference to his name. In conclusion, to quote the late military historian, General J.F.C. Fuller:

> Who first thought of propelling a ball through a metal tube by exploding gunpowder is unknown … anyhow it certainly was *not* monk Berthold Schwartz.

Mixing gunpowder, c. fifteenth century. Note how it is being sifted by the man on the right and the man on the left is grinding it into a fine powder.

ARTILLERY IN EUROPE: THE CRÉCY PERIOD

The Battle of Crécy, 26 August 1346, is very important in European history, not least because it was the first major land battle in a series of many engagements fought between France and England over an extended period commonly referred to as the Hundred Years War. It is also recognized as being the first authenticated account of a battle where an English army used gunpowder in battle. The war, which actually lasted 116 years, from 1337 to 1453, broke out following a typical feudal dispute. The Hundred Years War did not consist of continuous fighting, but can instead be categorized into eight periods, with lengths of uneasy peace existing in-between as a result of various treaties. The first episode is known as the Crécy Period, lasting between 1345 and 1347. For several years the two countries had clashed in a number of relatively minor engagements, as a result of Edward III entering France, establishing military bases and proclaiming himself King of France, before the two armies faced one another across a field just outside the small town of Crécy.

On 26 August 1346 the army of Edward III comprised some 3,000 men-at-arms and knights, 10,000 archers and a number of others serving as infantrymen. The French army numbered some 60,000 troops, of whom 12,000 were heavy cavalry, supported with a mercenary force of some 6,000 Genoese crossbowmen, commanded by Odone Doria and Carlo Grimaldi. The weather was inclement and there had been a brief but intense rainstorm shortly before the opening of the battle, which was to have disastrous consequences for the French. The French with their numerical superiority were confident of success and proceeded to stage one cavalry charge after another. Despite their heavy armour protection each successive assault was halted and broken by the withering hail of arrows put up by the force of archers in Edward's army. Armed with the longbow, even the most inexperienced archer was capable of shooting at least six arrows per minute, while very experienced archers could shoot up to ten arrows per minute, to produce a veritable 'storm of arrows', which was more than sufficient to halt even the most determined cavalry charge. The Genoese crossbowmen attempted to return fire but the range was too long for their crossbow arrows to carry and the rain had slackened the strings of their weapons which further reduced the range of their arrows. The English archers had kept their bowstrings dry during the rainstorm and were able to shoot a deadly hail of arrows against the Genoese troops who broke rank and fled.

Apart from the longbow, Edward III had another secret weapon in his ranks in the shape of gunpowder artillery. The exact number of pieces of artillery deployed by the English is uncertain, with the chronicler Mezeray, for example, recording that Edward 'struck terror into the French army with five or six pieces of cannon, it being the first time they had seen such thundering machines'. Whatever the strength of Edward's artillery, it is the presence of these weapons which the Italian chronicler, Villani, blames for causing the failure of the Genoese crossbowmen to remain at their posts. Villani states that Edward sited his artillery among the ranks of his archer's positions and describes their effect as being 'most fearful'. Another account states that these pieces 'with fire throw little balls to frighten and destroy horses'. This is rather significant because, although artillery had been known in Europe for more than thirty years, and even used in some military actions, no direct reference had been made to its presence on the battlefield influencing the outcome of the engagement.

The weapons themselves are sometimes referred to as being either 'bombards' or 'roundelades', terms for weapons in use at the time. However, it is interesting to note that Villani refers to them as 'cannons', a modern term which has been Anglicized in the translation from the original Italian manuscript, where they are called *cannone*. As the years passed, this expression would become more widely used so that it encompassed all pieces of gunpowder artillery.

No one knows for certain the exact form of those weapons used by Edward's army. At this stage of development of artillery in Europe the weapons could have been firing balls of stone, lead or iron, or even the arrow-like projectile as depicted in early manuscripts. Another unknown factor is the method of manufacture of the weapons themselves. They could have been single-piece castings or manufactured using the 'hoop and stave' method of construction, both processes known to be in use at the time to produce the elongated tube-like shape. We know these methods of manufacture were possible from excavations that have uncovered one of the earliest known cannons from an archaeological site in China. It has been tentatively dated to 1288 and consists of a cast-iron barrel surrounded by several strengthening bands. The device is one metre in length and has a calibre of just over 25mm and may have been mounted on a pivot. From this design the Chinese also developed the stackened or hoop and stave method of constructing the barrels of cannons.

Edward's artillery would have lacked wheels, with each weapon being moved into its firing position by a wagon. On removal from the wagon, the weapon would have been fastened to a simple trestle rest, known as a 'talaria', which was often very roughly hewn. This would control the weapon during firing and provide elevation to the barrel. The construction of the weapons would have meant that they were extremely heavy, with a very slow rate of fire. On the right flank of Edward's position was a windmill and records are consistent in stating that he used this as a command post. Some believe that his artillery was sited in a position some 300yd in front of this building, which would indeed place the weapons among the ranks of his archers on the Black Prince's right flank and support the records of Villani. Due to their bulk it is unlikely that the weapons would have been moved once they were emplaced.

The English gunfire at the Battle of Crécy is recorded as having:

cast iron balls by means of fire ... They made a

sound (noise) like thunder and caused much loss in men and horses

However, these weapons would have fired only a few times during the battle. In view of what Froissart records of the engagement, and the limited power of the cannons, it is unlikely that they alone would have demoralized the enemy. In fact, considering the limited range and poor accuracy of such early artillery it appears that Villani may have been seeking excuses for the lack of moral fibre shown by his fellow countrymen in battle. Indeed, Froissart in his version of events, states that Edward's cannons made but 'two or three discharges on the Genosese'.

Actually, given the fact that a number of chroniclers, such as Villani, Mezeray, Monstrelet and Froissart, recorded events surrounding the actions of the Hundred Years War, it is interesting to note that very little direct reference is made to gunpowder artillery during the early phase of this episodic period. Indeed, it is only in the second half of the protracted fighting that artillery is mentioned in a more prominent aspect, as it begins to take on a more tactical role in battle. Even so, little reference, if any, is made to the men who served these weapons and the methods that they used to load and fire the cannons. As a result, we do not know how many men were required to operate each cannon, nor anything about their background and how they came to learn the art of shooting with gunpowder artillery.

According to various sources, the French launched fifteen or sixteen separate attacks at Crécy before finally giving up and leaving over 1,500 knights and in excess of 10,000 men-at-arms and infantrymen dead on the field of battle. A realistic examination of the casualty figures for the battle makes it hard to believe that Edward III's artillery could have caused even a small percentage of these deaths. It is highly likely that the gunfire did unnerve the horses, which would have been difficult enough to control under the storm of arrows. The average daily usage of gunpowder per weapon at this time has been calculated as being somewhere in the order of only 300g (10¹/₂oz), which raises the question of why would any army want to deploy heavy and cumbersome weaponry which lacked mobility and could be unreliable in use. The answer is really quite simple, that whichever side possesses advanced weaponry will use it, especially if it is believed that it may influence the outcome of a battle. It is probable that this alone was enough to guarantee its use, even though the weapons absorbed great amounts of time, manpower and money. In 1850, just over 500 years after the Battle of Crécy, an excavation around the site revealed an iron cannon ball of 250mm (9³/₄in) diameter. Some historians claimed that this was conclusive proof of artillery in the army of Edward III. However, it is unlikely that the artillery of the time could have fired such a projectile, and besides which metal would surely have been a resource too valuable to waste when stone shot would suffice.

This leads to the conclusion that the excavated cannonball must have come from a much later period.

THE ARTILLERY ARMS RACE

The term artillery has long been used by armies, a tradition carried over into the medieval period, when it was applied to the whole range of siege engines. These devices used either tension or torsion energy to propel the projectiles used to bombard the target castle or town during a siege. This range of weaponry included a machine known as the trebuchet, the only such device to be invented during the Middle Ages, which used the counterpoise system for propelling its payload. Some of the larger of these weapons could hurl payloads of up to 100kg (220lb) over ranges of 200m (or yards), which was far in excess of anything that

Stone cannon ball of the type used in the fourteenth century.

Roughly hewn stone cannon ball of the type used in the fourteenth century.

Large stone cannon ball which would have been shaped by a stonemason.

Artillery of the fourteenth century being fired from a platform which has a device to adjust the elevation of the barrel – very rudimentary and apparently not of a stout design. It could well be that this is an artist's impression created by someone who had not seen the actual weapon.

could be fired from early gunpowder weapons. It was only natural that the same term should be applied to gunpowder weapons because, after all, these new weapons were only continuing in the same role as the catapults and mangonols. The only real difference between the two types of weapons is the fact that cannons used chemical energy, in the form of propelling gasses created by the burning of gunpowder, to hurl the projectiles, whereas the older weapons used mechanical energy. It is known that by about the time of the first half of the fourteenth century, the limited numbers of small cannons in service with the armies of some western European countries were being used alongside traditional siege equipment such as the trebuchet. The appearance of gunpowder weapons, in effect, caused an arms race in which no country or state could afford to lag behind.

Only four years after the Battle of Crécy, the chronicler Petrarch, in 1350, described the presence of cannons on the battlefield as being 'as common and familiar as other kinds of arms'. Admittedly, in that same year the Pope's army in Rome is known to have raised its own force of gunpowder artillery, and so Petrarch's statement should perhaps not be taken at face value. The appearance of new developments in the shape of cannon must have prompted such exaggerated exclamations of this nature. But once invented and deployed, it must be accepted that the increase in the use of cannons would have been inexorable but relatively slow. The slow growth in the spread of artillery was due to a number of factors, not the least of which was expense. There was also the time taken to train men to fire these weapons, the problems of transportation and the gathering in of resources necessary for the manufacture of the weapons.

References to the range of weapons using the properties of gunpowder to propel a projectile appear to be more widespread in Europe than in the Far East. This may be because such weapons were being used by more than one country. Even so, the full power of artillery on the battlefield was not to be completely realized until the end of the Middle Ages. Although the Battle of Crécy may be proof positive of the use of artillery on the battlefield, it is believed that it had actually been present on the European continent for almost twenty years. This view is supported by Lieutenant Colonel Henry Hime, a British officer serving in the Royal Artillery, in his work *The Origins of Artillery*, in which he points to the fact that Edward III of England had used artillery in his campaign against the Scots in 1327 and 1328, where they were termed 'crakys of war'. On discharge, the noise made by these cannons was like nothing the Scots had ever heard before. Like all deployment of artillery on the battlefield at this time, its use was not conclusive to the outcome of any one engagement during the time of the campaign, but it left an indelible impression on those who witnessed it. Following a skirmish at Weardale, for example, John Barbour, the Archdeacon of Aberdeen, was moved to record the events in *The Metrical Life of King Robert Bruce*:

Twa noveltyes that day thai saw
That forouth in Scotland has been nane:
Tymmris for helmyss was the ane,
That they brought then of great beautie,
And also wonder for to see
The other crakys were of war
That thai before heard never air

This, it should be remembered, was at a time when the loudest noise heard in everyday life is likely to have been a clap of thunder or the tolling of a bell. The skirmish at Weardale occurred during the period of Robert The Bruce, who was born in 1275, before the advent of gunpowder weapons, and died in 1329, only one year after the use of gunpowder

artillery in that skirmish. Thus Robert the Bruce is likely to have had only limited personal experience of gunpowder artillery. Another pre-eminent figure of the age was Bertrand du Guesclin, born in 1320, at a time before the widespread use of gunpowder weapons. Born into a family of minor French nobility, du Guesclin was an unconventional military leader who eventually became the Constable of France, making him the most powerful man in the country after the king. He was a forward-thinking figure who employed battlefield tactics previously unheard of in western Europe. In fact, such was his influence that a phase of the Hundred Years War, from 1368, has been termed after him. He quickly learned about the power of artillery, which he incorporated into his tactics when he mounted offensive campaigns against the English. He further added to the changing face of war by introducing the 'scorched earth' policy, a tactic which denied the enemy any means of living off the land, and by raising specialist artillery units. He also refused to give battle if the situation did not meet with his satisfaction. By the time of his death on the field of battle, in 1380, during the siege of Randon, gunpowder artillery was being commonly deployed on the battlefield and armies had come to depend on its presence in their ranks to provide them with an increased chance of victory.

In the first half of the fourteenth century, armies had been slow, almost to the point of reluctance, to deploy gunpowder artillery on the battlefield. No doubt this had been part of the chivalrous code of knightly conduct, but once it was decided that such weapons should be used in battle, warfare would never be the same again. Regardless of his armour, gunpowder reduced the chivalrous knight to the same vulnerable status as the common foot soldier, in the same way that castles of the pre-gunpowder age were to be rendered obsolete. Despite the fact that there is irrefutable proof of artillery being present during a small number of battles and sieges in the first quarter of the fourteenth century, apart from a few casual references, there are remarkably few direct remarks made as to their actual efficacy during a military action.

Range of calibres showing varying sizes of stone cannon balls, to fit different weapons.

By this time the properties of gunpowder, or black powder, as it was termed due to its high charcoal content, had been known in Europe for almost 100 years. Despite this, the first recognizable cannons only began to appear in Europe around the turn of the thirteenth century. The point of entry into Europe and the origin of these weapons are not entirely clear. However, it is known that between 1306 and 1308, Ferdinand IV of Castile is understood to have driven the Moors out of Gibraltar by means of gunpowder artillery. By around *c.* 1314, artillery is recorded as being in use in Flanders. In fact archives kept at Ghent, and dating from 1313, record the use of *bussen met kruyt* which has been translated to mean 'cannon with powder'. Several years later a small number of devices had been shipped to England, which would place them in service for sufficient time to permit them to be deployed by Edward III in his campaign against the Scots. By 1339 the Scots had acquired suffi-

cient experience and pieces of artillery to use them in the siege of Stirling Castle. By the time of the reign of Robert II, 1370 to 1390, the Scots had built up a substantial artillery force including 'small cannons' in service, which had been successfully deployed in localized actions.

The earliest known illustration of artillery in use dates from 1326, at about the time when such weapons were known to be in limited use in France. The illustration shows a knightly figure engaged in the act of applying a lighted taper or match to the vent of what has been identified as being an early cannon. The device is mounted on a trestle-like table and is vase-shaped with a bulbous end. This early representation appears in the manuscript *De Nobilitatibus, Sapientiis, et Prudentiis Regum* (On the Majesty, Wisdom and Prudence of Kings), one of two volumes written by Walter de Millimete for Edward III. There is no explanatory text to accompany the illustration, but it may be

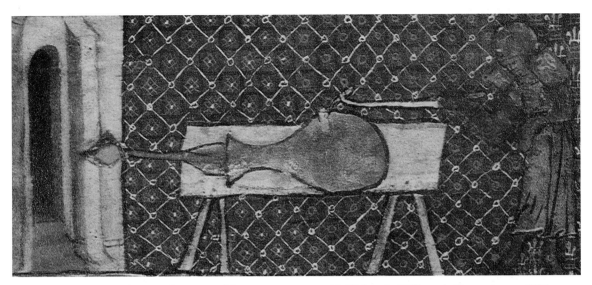

Part of the manuscript showing the image of the weapon portrayed in Walter de Millimete's illustration, c. 1326. It shows a rudimentary vase or bell-shaped barrel resting on a table just about to be fired.

dated by the dedication inscription on the title page. This document may, in turn, be based on a report telling of the use of such devices referred to variously as *vassi, pots de feu* (pots of fire), or *pots de fer* (pots of iron), which had been used at the Battle of Metz in 1324. In fact, gunpowder artillery may have been first used in Europe in this engagement against the king of Bohemia. The weapon portrayed in the Millimete manuscript is sometimes referred to as a 'tulip' gun because of its profile. It would appear to be made from cast bronze, an alloy made from combining copper and tin to produce a very strong material which will not corrode. Its very appearance leads one to conclude that it was almost certainly cast in a bell foundry, where the expertise and knowledge to handle such volumes of molten metal existed. The muzzle or front end of the barrel is shown flared, but the actual bore from which the projectile was fired is very small. Modern experiments involving recreated weapons of this type indicate that the bore was between 25mm and 30mm (0.97 to 1.17in). This small calibre would have permitted only leather bound iron arrows to be loaded for firing.

Further Developments

In February 1326, twenty years before the Battle of Crécy and only one year before the commencement of Edward's campaign against the Scots, a significant development took place. In Florence, records reveal that the Signoria of the city had set aside sufficient funds to purchase brass cannons and iron balls. Furthermore, the Priors, Gonfalonier and twelve others were authorized to secure such 'for the defence of the commune, camps and territory of Florence', and two men were appointed to make 'iron bullets and iron arrows for canones de metallo'. In Italy terms such as *maestro delle bombarde* (master of the bombard) were being used to define those capable of using gunpowder artillery. Within five years of the decree of Florence in 1326, weapons called *vasa* were being used by Prussian troops during attacks against the town of Cividale in Friaul in 1331. In 1366 the Prussians had taken further examples of artillery to Italy, where the weapons became adopted by local armies. In fact during the War of Chioggia, 1379–1380, between the Venetians and

A recreated weapon in the style of that shown in the Walter de Millimete illustration, c. 1326. This is on display at Fort Nelson in Fareham, Hampshire where it forms part of the Royal Armouries exhibition. It shows the heavy, cumbersome design of the earliest known gunpowder artillery weapon. It has been recreated using only images and written references. Even so, it is a good representation of how the original weapon must have looked.

Genoese, both sides made considerable use of artillery including the types known as bombards. In January 1380, for example, the Venetians deployed a number of bombards to lay siege to the monastery of Brondolo, built in a style comparable to a castle of the period. The Venetian cannons fired stone balls weighing 200lb (90kg) and the battery is believed to have fired at least 140 such projectiles during the action, one of which struck the campanile and killed twenty-two men.

THE GUNNERS

But what of the men who loaded and fired the cannons? Despite the existence of early written documents making references to the actual weapons and some of the actions, apart from some brief accounts relating by name to a particular person responsible for the storage of the artillery, very little is known. For example, who manufactured the weapons and gunpowder and how was this knowledge transferred? With very little written work being produced at the time, most information would have been passed on by word of mouth or by direct contact with the events taking place. It is possible that the first workshops producing cannons may have also produced the gunpowder, as a group of artisans working in conjunction with one another. As such, their skills would have been in great demand and this would have placed them in a position which allowed them to negotiate favourable terms regarding payment. This is borne out by later writings, in which are recorded details of 'contracts of services' which guarantee payment and protection extended to the family of the gunner or cannoneer. But as to whom these artillerists were and where they worked is something of a mystery. Gunners were regarded as a class apart from other troops, and it took courage to be a cannoneer, not least because they were thought to be in league with the devil. Some accounts go as far as stating that gunners did not participate in plunder and drinking when on campaign. This may well be correct, because they would have needed

their wits about them in order to prevent accidents when handling gunpowder and to protect their cannons.

It is known from accounts that the artillery force that Edward III took with him to France was very well organized, with a logistics supply running back to England. This we know from his Keeper of the Tower Wardrobe, Robert de Mildenhall, who oversaw the assembling of an artillery train for Edward's invasion of France in 1345. We also know that re-supplies were to be sent from England, but exactly where such materials originated is still unknown. Not until the fifteenth century would written documents be produced to allow us to answer such matters. Records from the period do explain something of Edward's military forces in 1344, among which is listed 'Ingyners lvii;

Recreated fifteenth-century gunner as at the time of the Wars of the Roses. Note gunners' loading tools to rear of picture. These include wooden rammers and ladles.

Artillery is used to attack a castle. Note the basic means of elevating the barrel.

artillers vi; gonners vi'. The figure of six gunners and six artillerymen would indeed match the possible number of guns deployed on the field at Crécy. This may not seem a large number, but it should be remembered that these would have been master gunners and that the labourers employed to pull the guns and carry the shot and powder would not be listed. These experts in their field would have probably been under some form of contract to the King, who is also known to have had in his employ Peter van Vullaere, who had at one time been the 'Master of Ribauldequins' (*maitre de ribaudequins*) at the city of Bruges.

LOADING THE AMMUNITION

All the weapons at this time were of a design which today is termed 'muzzle loaded'. That is to say, the gunpowder was first inserted into the barrel from the muzzle end and rammed down into the enclosed chamber or breech end of the barrel. After this a projectile was inserted, either in the form of a leather-bound iron arrow or, as in later weapons, a small round stone or a lead pellet. A small hole, later termed the vent, connected the powder chamber to the outside of the barrel. To fire the weapon, a man simply applied a burning ember or inserted a piece of heated metal to the touch hole (an

expression derived from the French term *touché*) to ignite the powder in the chamber. Aiming was rudimentary and amounted to no more than pointing the weapon in the desired direction. Very little was understood about the science of gunpowder and, on firing, the weapon would have been virtually impossible to control. Muzzle-loading artillery weapons were to remain in service until well into the nineteenth century.

Much is known about the muzzle-loading method because this operation stayed in practice and unchanged for an extremely long period. The loading operation would have been a slow process, requiring great care and attention. First a man would insert a quantity of gunpowder into the barrel using long-handled wooden ladles or scoops. This was followed by a bundle of rag, cloth, straw or grass, known as the 'wad', the purpose of which was to keep the powder compact. The powder and wadding were then well rammed using another long-handled wooden device. Once this procedure had been completed, a ball of stone, iron or lead would be inserted and rammed down until well seated on the powder. This was a dangerous operation because if a gap was left between the ball and the powder, air could penetrate, permitting a build up of pressure which could cause the barrel to explode. A small amount of gunpowder was then applied to the touch hole or vent. A hot iron or ember was used to ignite this, setting up a flash to ignite the main charge in the chamber. Before the weapon could be reloaded, the barrel had to swabbed out with a bundle of wet rags or wool on a long wooden pole. This was to remove any unburned powder and extinguish any remaining powder which might still be smouldering, which could otherwise lead to a premature explosion when powder was placed in the barrel.

It was usually left to the master gunner's judgement to decide how much powder to load for a specific weight of shot. It was only through trial and error over the years that the required charge of powder would become fully understood and the loading procedure turned into an exact science. In fact, it was not until the fifteenth century that the first reliable written instructions appeared, and even then circulation of this information was strictly controlled. However, it is interesting to note that the loading and firing sequence as first formulated was to remain as standard practice, requiring only slight refinements over the years. Indeed, the action was virtually unaltered until the turn of the eighteenth century, when specially prepared bagged charges of gunpowder were introduced, a move which greatly speeded up the loading process and made the handling of gunpowder much safer.

DEVELOPMENTS IN CHINA

During this period the design of cannon was undergoing a transitional stage not only in Europe but also in China. Indeed, such is the way in which the technologies of the two such diverse cultures appeared to parallel one another, that one is inclined to ponder just who copied who at this stage in the arms development race? One Chinese piece of this time was referred to as the 'thousand-ball thunder cannon' and illustrations of the period show these weapons being used in a similar manner to those in Europe at the same time. Written works on artillery would not appear in China until the fifteenth century. A work called *The Fire-Drake Artillery Manual*, dated around 1412, men-

tions one particular cannon referred to as the 'long-range awe-inspiring cannon', which weighed some 72kg (160lb). Whilst not particularly heavy in itself, this weapon could be loaded with a single lead ball weighing 1.2kg ($2^1/_2$lb) or a sack containing up to 100 small lead balls and was fired by a charge of 250g ($8^3/_4$oz) of powder. This is comparable to the capabilities of most European weapons at the same time. The latter type of multiple projectile load also had its counterparts in Europe where fragments of scrap metal would be loaded for firing as an anti-personnel charge at close range. Known at the time as 'langridge', it would eventually be refined into loads known as 'canister' and 'grape shot'.

CONFUSION SURROUNDING THE USE OF THE TERM ARTILLERY

Although a number of accounts mentioning artillery were recorded by chroniclers, there is some discrepancy surrounding the actual terms and translation of records over the years. Therefore, one cannot always accept the term of artillery in the literal sense of the word, and confusion arises when reference is made regarding artillery prior to the first half of the fourteenth century. This point is illustrated by the Chronicles written by Grafton, which record the events of a dangerous revolt which erupted in London during 1267. The Earl of Gloucester had made serious threats against the King, and moved to usurp the regency of Henry III, who was absent from the city at the time. The King knew he had to crush this outbreak of dissent, and he marched on the city to engage Gloucester and reassert his power. It is at this point that some confusion arises, because it appears that he may have had gunpowder artillery in his train. Grafton's Chronicles from the time state that the King was 'making daily assaults when guns and other ordnance were shot into the city', but the exact type and nature of this artillery is not recorded. Because of the lack of further notes to corroborate the records, Grafton's references have come to be seen as less than reliable and may have possibly been distorted over the years by later historians. In view of this, it is probable that Grafton's references should be taken as implying that the artillery used by Henry III was a range of contemporary weapons using a mixture of torsion- and tension-powered siege engines such as the catapult and mangonol, which were commonly used during sieges at the time. If incendiary weapons were used, it is more likely that they were of the type based on the design of the so-called 'thunder balls' (*chen t'ien lei*), examples of which may have been left behind in Europe by the Mongols when they retreated in 1242. These spherical devices were filled with a basic gunpowder compound and launched from catapults using torsion power. It may be that Grafton's references to such tactics may have been misinterpreted over the years.

Another example of this confusion is to be found in Colonel Chesney's book *Observations of Firearms*, in 1852, in which he states how:

> The Moors, according to Conde [a high authority on this subject] used artillery against Saragossa in 1118; and in 1132 a culverin of four pounds calibre, named Salamonica, was made.

In 1157, when the Spaniards took Niebla, the Moors defended themselves with machines that threw darts and stones by means of fire. The Moorish king, Abd' almumen, is credited with having captured Mohadia, a fortified city near Bona, from the Sicilians, by the same means. In 1280, artillery is recorded as having been used in action at Cordova, but again this is probably a reference to torsion engines of the time. Admittedly, gunpowder devices are known to have been in use in China at this time, but it is unlikely that they were of sufficiently advanced design to win wars and battles. Therefore, one has to conclude that Colonel Chesney and other historians recording these twelfth-century engagements may have been making the same mistake as Grafton and their contemporaries in simply taking the term artillery at face value and to mean gunpowder weapons.

CONFLICTS IN THE HUNDRED YEARS WAR

In 1337, at the time of the outbreak of the Hundred Years War, few people, including soldiers, had ever directly encountered gunpowder weapons. In fact the dominant figure on the battlefield, certainly in the case of the English army, was the archer with his longbow. A well-trained archer could outshoot, in both range and accuracy, those types of gunpowder weapons that existed at the time. In fact it would be nearly another 200 years before the longbow ceased to be the principal shock weapon used by the English army in warfare. Fighting between England and France swayed backwards and forwards, with short periods of peace following truces, during which time each side would withdraw to recover and recoup their losses in men and re-equip with the latest weaponry, which happened to include cannon.

The year of 1338 was something of a turning point in warfare, with the French showing just how versatile artillery could be when used in an imaginative way. One of their military actions involved mounting an amphibious assault against the English port of Southampton, where they succeeded in setting fire to the town and sacking it. Among the weaponry of the raiding party, sailing from Harfleur, was a single 'bottle-shaped' gunpowder weapon known as either a *ribaud* or *pot de fer*, equipped with forty-eight arrow-shaped iron projectiles and approximately 3lb (1.4kg) of gunpowder. Receipts for the range of weaponry exist at the Bibliotheque Nationale in Paris. The French action against Southampton is proof to support that such a weapon capable of firing arrow-like projectiles, as seen in the manuscript by Walter de Milimete, just over ten years previously, actually existed. With this action the French proved that artillery could be used from ships to mount surprise attacks against coastal targets. In the same year the French used similar weapons to protect the town of Rouen and fired leather-bound iron arrows against the attackers. The types of weapons used from ships were identical to those deployed in land battles.

This was to remain the normal practice for several hundred years, until special designs were developed. The French were far more advanced than the English in the use of artillery at this time, and in 1339 they used artillery to attack the English stronghold of Puy Guillem in the Perigord. By 1340, they used 'canons et bombards' to fire iron arrows at the English at an engagement at Quesnoy.

At the time of the French attack in 1338, artillery is understood to have been present in England for almost twenty years, but it is not until that year that the first English reference is made to gunpowder artillery. In that year the Keeper of the King's Ships received a contract to deliver 'ij (2) canons de ferr'. The inventory goes on to include: 'un canon de fer ove II cambers un autre de bras ove un chamber'. This request may have come as a direct result of the French action at Southampton, and certainly by 1347 English ships were also mounting cannon. In 1345, Edward III instructed the Keeper of the Tower Wardrobe (The Tower of London), Robert de Mildenhall, to assemble a force of 100 ribaulds (ribauldequins), for which purpose he was authorized to collect timber, wheels, axles and other materials. This move was in preparation for Edward's invasion of France, which in addition to the ribaulds included another twenty pieces of artillery. He used these against the city of Calais and his lines of communications meant that he could dispatch his fleet of ships back to England to transport re-supplies of powder and further weapons. Although termed Keeper of the Tower Wardrobe, Robert de Mildenhall was responsible for issuing arms and ammunition, and his records show in 1346 he also dispatched '73 large lead shot, 31 small lead shot and six pieces of lead' for the King to use at Calais. Furthermore, according to a writ dated 10 May 1346, only five months before the Battle of Crécy, de Mildenhall also sent out '912lb of saltpetre, and 846lb of sulphur', which would allow Edward's gunners to make gunpowder. However, Edward was forced to leave most of these supplies and weapons behind,

Recreated, triple-barrelled ribauldequin. This was a light field gun intended for close-quarter fighting and would have inflected serious injury to those in the path of the projectiles.

Original ribauldequin with twelve barrels. This fired projectiles in a wide pattern and would have been used at close quarters. It would have been devastating against infantry and would have inflicted wounds to several ranks deep.

because of their size and weight, when he advanced further into the French countryside. These actions illustrate perfectly how neither country could afford to fall behind in the arms race that had developed between France and England.

By 1346, the Hundred Years War was already nearly ten years in the fighting, and at the time of the Battle of Crécy in the same year, the use of gunpowder artillery was showing signs of spreading. The early battles in which gunpowder weapons were used had yielded mixed results, but they had set the pattern by which all subsequent wars would be fought. Some countries, such as England and Switzerland, would for a time resist complete transition to gunpowder weaponry and instead put faith in tried and tested battlefield tactics and traditional weapons. For example, during the opening phases of the Hundred Years War the English army

is believed to have had only fifteen cannons in service and a store of less than 90lb (40kg) of black powder. On the other hand, countries such as France and Spain realized the potency of such weaponry and very early on became leaders in its use. Eventually, the Swiss and English would come to realize the folly of their ways and adopt cannons and other firearms in favour of longbows and halbards.

DESIGN OF EARLY WEAPONS AND PROJECTILES

Arrow-Shaped Projectiles

The firing of leather-bound arrow-shaped projectiles was widely spread, but their shape meant they were most suited for use against personnel. Such projectiles lacked weight and their relatively small size meant that they were incapable of inflicting any real damage to the walls surrounding castles or towns. But this did not prevent them from being used by many countries, including China. In fact, in Russia all-iron arrow-shaped projectiles some 2m in length are recorded as being in use against the city of Vladimir. In 1340, for example, accounts for the city of Lille record how payment was made to Jehan Piet de Fur 'pour III tuaiux de tonnaire et pour cent garros, VI livres XVI sous ...' ('for three tubes of thunder and 100 arrows'). During the siege of Artois castle at Rihoult in 1342, arrow-shaped projectiles were fired from cannons. Further direct reference to artillery in another battle during the same year tells how King Alfonso of Castile used an unknown number of artillery pieces at the siege of Algeciras.

Pots de Fer

Early gunpowder weapons in fourteenth-century Europe were very basic, almost to the point of being crude, by any standards. They were unreliable, inaccurate and very difficult to control during firing. As we have seen, they comprised little more than a simple vase- or bell-shaped device with a thickened base into which was bored a small hole that connected to that part of the weapon containing the gunpowder, termed the chamber. It is on this point that a discrepancy arises, because some researchers do not believe the touch hole was available until after 1375. The significance of this date is not entirely clear, but the small hole in the base to permit the firer to insert a hot iron to ignite the powder charge is to be seen in the 1326 de Milimete manuscript. It is also repeated in another chronicle known as the Holkham Hall manuscript, which also dates from *c.* 1326, which has been examined and authenticated as being genuine. If, as the detractors assert, the early weapons did not have touch holes to permit ignition of the gunpowder, then exactly how were they fired? No other method of firing has been put forward, and so it is clear that touch holes must have existed even on the first gunpowder weapons.

The earliest devices are shown with flared muzzles, but the actual size or calibre of the opening from which the projectile was fired was really quite narrow. Evidence has emerged that the first projectiles for these early artillery pieces were no more than large arrows, the shafts of which were bound in leather to fit into the barrel, which was between 50mm and 75mm (2–3in) diameter. The smaller weapons would probably have been placed in shallow dips in the ground from where they would have been fired, which would have done nothing for accuracy or controllability. Indeed, as recounted by the chroniclers, these early gunpowder weapons were simply used to produce loud noises to startle the enemy and their horses. At the Battle of Quesnoy in 1340, for example, Froissart records how the French bombards *jetoient grands carreaux* fired at the English with great noise. However, on that occasion it was the French horses which stampeded and became uncontrollable.

Examples of such *pots de fer* have been uncovered at sites of archaeological diggings, such as Loshult in Sweden, which was excavated in 1861. The site cannot be dated with absolute accuracy due to lack of supporting evidence, but the appearance of the weapons agrees with the shape of devices shown in manuscripts of the time. This has led to some archaeologists prescribing a tentative date at around mid to late fourteenth century, say 1350–1375. Similar devices found at other battle sites vary in size from those capable of being emplaced by a single person to larger, unwieldy, weapons, which would have required three or four people to lift them into place. These larger cannons would have been secured to some form of platform, almost certainly more substantial that that shown in the de Milimete manuscript, and pointed directly at the intended target, which was usually a castle or town under siege. The weapon may have been angled to provide some form of elevation for some extra range, and aiming would have amounted to no more than simple line of sight. In other words, if they could see the target they fired the cannons directly at it. It is very likely that, at this early stage in the history of artillery, there was no real scientific approach to its use.

There are several possible reasons why weapons may have been discarded on the battlefield. The user of the weapon might have been killed, and because other troops were not experienced in the use of such weapons it was simply left where it fell. Another possibility is that after firing his entire supply of gunpowder, an inexperienced gunner might see no sense in carrying a weapon that could no longer be fired. Whatever the reason, more experienced troops using these cannons would not have thrown them away indiscriminately because they would have been aware of the huge cost of manufacturing the weapons and their importance to their King or field commander. Also, as experts in the use of gunpowder weapons they would have been classed as an elite group. In fact, rather than being killed on capture, there is every possibility that such skilled men would have been offered inducements to fight for the side that offered the highest rate of pay.

The first weapons were cast from bronze and, as historians such as Dudley Pope have expounded, could well have been manufactured at bell foundries. The shape and compact size of the smaller designs made them relatively simple to use, if in a somewhat unpredictable manner. Gunnery in the fourteenth century was still in its infancy and being practised by men who understood little of the power they had within their grasp. When fired at a target the size of a castle or city it was hard to miss, and the projectile would cause damage at the point of impact by virtue of its sheer weight and kinetic energy, if it struck hard enough. But the projectiles did not necessarily kill the occupants of the building, as a poem of the period entitled 'The Ballard of the Battle of Crecy' tells:

Gonners to schew their art
Into the town in many a part
Schote many a great full stone.
Thanked be God and Mary mild,

They hurt neyther man, woman nor child;
To the houses, though, they did great harm.

Stone and Iron Projectiles

At first the projectiles were stone balls shaped by masons, who made use of the plentiful and usually readily available stocks of stone at the site of a siege. These projectiles were round, but their size was not consistent and they were often a poor fit for the barrel. The result was that the projectile frequently did not reach the target or lacked sufficient energy to create lasting damage. Poorly fitting stone projectiles also meant that a lot of powder was blasted from the weapon without imparting any propellant force to the projectile. Furthermore, stone projectiles tended to smash upon coming into contact with thick, unyielding, castle walls. Whilst this did little damage to the fabric of the castle's wall, the stone splinters inflicted anti-personnel injuries to the defenders, which reduced the garrison. Later on, iron projectiles would smash the walls more effectively, but size for size the heavier iron projectiles required considerably more gunpowder than stone projectiles. However, iron projectiles could be cast to a consistent calibre to produce a better fit into the barrel, which in turn produced improved powder efficiency and reduced loss of blast.

Bombards

The range of weapons known as bombards were made in a variety of sizes and could be either muzzle loaded or breech loaded. They were usually best suited to siege warfare, where their large calibre projectiles could be directed against castles or walled towns. One explanation of the origin of the term 'bombard' is that it came from the humming buzz set up by the projectile when fired. However, the more probable origin is that it came from the Italian expression *bombo et ardore*, meaning thunder and lightning. Bombards were transported to the designated site of use by horse-drawn carts and deployed either directly on the ground or mounted on a specially constructed wooden platform, called a telaria. The former method provided little, if any, control of the weapon during firing, while the telaria did, at least, afford some margin of stability. The rear end or breech of the barrel was butted up against stout baulks of timber which had been hammered into the ground in order to provide a secure frame to absorb the recoil force when it was fired. Dragging such large and heavy weapons around the battlefield was not considered tactically important and it was a labour-intensive chore which required the services of troops who could otherwise be put to other use on the battlefield. Lacking wheels, it would have required the services of many men, using ropes and levers, to haul the larger bombards, some of which measured between 4yd (3.7m) and 6yd (5.5m) in length with calibres between 15–18in (380mm and 460mm), from one site on the battlefield to another. Since they could not be easily be moved, they would

have been used to fire several shots during the opening stages of a battle before they were forced to hold fire in order to avoid hitting their own troops as the battle developed into a mêlée.

Breech Loaders

As the fourteenth century progressed, another form of weapon which required a different loading sequence from that of the earlier muzzle loaded cannons was developed. These weapons were of a design which today we know as breech loaders. That is to say the loading sequence took place at the rear or lower end of the barrel. This method of loading cannons is believed to have been developed in the 1370s. Some sources quote 1372 as the precise date when this method of loading first appeared. However, this is rather ambiguous, when the exact location of its invention and the date are not clearly defined. The early breech-

Large bombard firmly secured to a wooden frame known as a telaria. Note how well bolstered it is by wooden blocks. Also note the large stone balls for ammunition.

Large bombard in use at the siege of Randon in France, 1380. It shows archers firing at the target castle, which would have harassed the defenders while the bombard would have battered the walls.

loading cannons required that removable pots, not unlike large drinking mugs of the day, complete with a handle, be inserted into the open breech-end of the barrel and secured in place with a wooden wedge hammered into position. The pots themselves, known as 'thunder boxes', were in effect detachable chambers for the breech of the barrel. One of the larger versions of weapon to employ this type of loading method was referred to as the *veuglaire* or 'fowler'. Other, much

smaller versions, were called *crapaudeaux* or 'toads'.

These 'thunder boxes' were a great advantage to the gunners and could be pre-loaded with a charge of gunpowder and a wad between it and the cannonball, like a small barrel. This advancement in technology meant that such devices could be readied in advance of any actual fighting, which greatly increased the rate of fire. It became clear that if a number of such devices were prepared, and stored in dry conditions, they could be supplied by gunners serving a number of guns in order to maintain a relatively high rate of fire. In some cases, a good gun crew could fire at a rate approaching something in the order of one shot every four or five minutes to produce ten to fifteen shots per hour. This was much faster than anything that could be achieved with muzzle-loading weapons. The pre-loaded pots simply had to be inserted into the chamber, which was a trough-shaped opening at the breech-end of the barrel, and a wooden wedge hammered in to secure it into place. Priming powder was applied to the touch hole, and a heated iron used to ignite this and thus fire the main charge of powder. These pots were quite advanced castings for the day, incorporating a handle, for ease of lifting, along with the opening for the touch hole. On early examples, the thickness of the walls of some of these pre-loaded pots could be as much as $1\frac{1}{2}$ times the calibre of projectile it was designed to discharge. A further advantage was that the weapons could be unloaded for safety when not required.

Another design of breech-loading weapon, using the pre-loaded pot method, was a piece called a 'peterara', from the fact that it fired stone projectiles. The barrel was formed using the built-up hoop and stave method, but it was not an entirely satisfactory design because gas-proof sealing at the breech could not be achieved. On some examples the staves forming the barrel could separate on firing, a sign of either poor craftsmanship or too much powder being loaded into the 'thunder box'.

A Barrel is Made for a Cannon

Through archaeological excavations, such as those conducted at the Hessian castle at Tannenburg, which is known to have been destroyed by artillery fire in 1399, it is possible to build a clear picture of early cast bronze *pots de fer* weapons. From this and other sites where other similar devices have been unearthed, we can begin to estimate just how widely spread were gunpowder weapons, how they were used and also attempt to chart the evolution of their development. When the design of these weapons is compared to that of church bells, it is hard to escape the conclusion that it was more than just coincidence that influenced the design of these early weapons. This similarity has been noted by a number of military historians, including John Keegan, who mentions these observations in his book *A History of Warfare*, and presents the theory that in the early days of artillery development, bell foundries were used to cast the barrels. Bell foundry in Europe had been established as early as the eighth century and these artisans would have understood the difficulties involved in casting difficult shapes and how to handle large quantities of molten metal.

It was only natural that their skills should have been utilized. In turn, they produced a design of weapon from a casting mould which was of a familiar shape to them. However, instead of producing an item with relatively thin walls and a wide opening, as in the case of a bell, the casting had very thick sides

and the opening was a long narrow bore. At the thickened base end another, smaller, hole connected this tube to the outside, through which the firer could ignite the powder in the chamber. This manufacturing process was to last until the middle of the fourteenth century, when it became evident that it could not keep up with supply and demand. Eventually, the foundry men at the bell casting centres had to admit that the demands for ever-larger weapons, in increasing numbers, which called for ever-increasing amounts of molten metal to be poured as a single-piece casting, was a process beyond even their capabilities and their handling facilities. The problem meant that new and different technologies had to be employed to produce the larger weapons being called for by armies.

In order to overcome the problem, artillery designers were forced to turn to the craft of the coopers who were skilled in the art of making barrels using staves (strips of wood) to build up a tube-like container. Indeed, it has been opined that it was the similarity of form between a hollow barrel and the hollow tube of a cannon produced by the cooper's method which led to use of the term 'barrel' in relation to weapons. Although it took a number of years to perfect the process, by the latter half of the fourteenth century it was common practice to make a cannon by placing billets, or strips of heated iron, lengthwise around a wooden former, known as a mandrel, and hammering

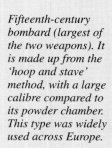

Fifteenth-century bombard (largest of the two weapons). It is made up from the 'hoop and stave' method, with a large calibre compared to its powder chamber. This type was widely used across Europe.

A Barrel is Made for a Cannon *continued*

them until they became welded together. Prior to being placed around the former, each billet iron had been worked by a blacksmith and could take many hours to form in the forge.

For greater strength these billets were secured in place with outer metal hoops, which had previously been heated to white-hot temperatures, and placed at points along the length of the billets. As the hoops cooled they contracted onto the formed tube of metal for greater strength. The whole structure was then placed in a fire and the wooden former burned away to leave a tube. The production of a cannon by this method of hammer-welding hot metal had to be carried out in stages, and could take a team of men many days to complete. Depending on the length of the barrel, some weapons could have between twenty-four and thirty-five outer hoops shrunk onto them, and further hammer welding applied. On some weapons these hoops were placed so closely together that they appeared as a complete outer casing for additional

Detail showing muzzle of recreated hoop and stave barrel weapon of the bombard type. The ropes shown here are to secure the barrel to the wheeled carriage.

Fifteenth-century wrought iron English gun, with the barrel built up in the hoop and stave method.

A Barrel is Made for a Cannon *continued*

Breech detail of recreated hoop and stave bombard. It is secured by a large baulk of wood and the carriage is mounted on wheels for ease of transport.

strength. It was a long, slow and laborious process requiring great skill, stamina and strength on the part of the metalworkers. The central mandrel was then removed and the cylindrical barrel of the cannon was ready.

Weapons manufactured in this method were known as either 'bar and bobbin' or 'hoop and stave' cannons. Another expression, used to a lesser degree, for a barrel made in this manner was that it was 'stackened' due to the fact that it resembled a sheath of stacked wheat. Not only did this new method of manufacture produce a weapon that was safer in use, but also meant that much larger guns could be built.

However, the drawback to this design was that the new manufacturing technique produced a barrel that

was open at both ends. In order to overcome this, a separate powder chamber had to be made. This was manufactured as a single-piece casting which was within the capabilities of metal foundries of the day. It had the appearance of a metal drinking tankard, complete with handle, and open at one end. Powder and shot could be loaded into the chamber before it was inserted into the rear or breech end of the barrel. It was secured in place by hammering wedges between the rear of the chamber and a vertical block of wood, which formed the rear end of the bed to which the barrel was firmly secured. This produced a weapon which had two chambers, which had long been seen in some quarters as the ideal design for a cannon. From the earliest days there were attempts to develop breech-loading weapons: the 'canon de fer ove II chambers'. Not only was it a safer way of loading the gunpowder, it also served to increase the number of times the weapon could be fired in quick succession. A number of these removable chambers could be prepared in advance, and provided they were stored in dry conditions, the cannon could be fired several times in fairly rapid succession by simply removing the empty chamber and replacing it with a loaded one. However, the design did not give a proper gas-tight seal at the breech end and some of the propelling gases would have vented out.

One style of weapon made in this manner was the bombard and these varied in size and in the weight of the projectile that they could fire. One weapon of this type was recovered from the moat during excavations at Bodiam Castle in Sussex, England, and was calculated to have required loading with a charge of 3lb (1.4kg) of black powder to fire a projectile of some 14.6in (370mm) in diameter. Records survive from 1377 which tell of a built-up cannon capable of firing a stone ball projectile weighing 200lb (90kg). It was built for the siege train of the Duke of Burgundy, and is known to have been used at the siege of Odruik. In the same year the records tell how the Duke ordered the building of a cannon capable of firing a 440lb (200kg) shot, which roughly equates to a calibre of 20in (510mm).

Another type of weapon built in this fashion was termed the 'petrarae' because it fired stone projectiles. It represented an improvement on the original concept, and had a barrel formed with metal arms or trough at the rear end into which the separate chamber could be dropped and wedged. The system was

A Barrel is Made for a Cannon *continued*

stronger than the separate-bed method and also permitted the complete weapon to be moved with some comparative ease. But in spite of the obvious advantages offered by such a firing method, the rudimentary methods of construction meant that the joint between the chamber and the barrel was far from gas tight. This meant that most of the explosive power vented out, thereby leading to a reduction in the velocity and range of the projectile, and posed a danger to the crew of the weapon. It is easy to suppose that the crew would have taken steps to develop some form of seal to reduce the danger to them and also to prevent the loss of propelling gases, perhaps by producing rings of leather cut to the correct size to at least reduce this effect. However, there is no documentary proof that this was ever done, so this remains pure supposition.

Certainly in Europe until the end of the sixteenth

Detail of muzzle of large English fifteenth-century hoop and stave muzzle-loaded bombard. The raised piece on the barrel is a sight, but it would have only shown the gunners a rough line to the target and the weapon would have remained inaccurate.

century the only metals available for use in making barrels were bronze or wrought iron. There was a great deal of variation in the way in which such metals were worked and this probably stems from the fact that local metal-working traditions were followed and the capability of blacksmiths ranged from adequate to very skilled. Bronze could be up to ten times as costly as wrought iron and was difficult to work, but it did have the advantage of being more durable and therefore lasting longer. In China during the fourteenth and fifteenth centuries cast bronze techniques and also cast iron were used to produce barrels that were cylindrical in shape, with slightly thickened, almost bulbous, breech ends. Known as *t'ungs* or *t'sungs*, they were some 600mm to 700mm (23–27in) in length, and used in a fashion similar to the device shown in the Walter de Milimete manuscript dated 1326.

The manufacture of a barrel for a cannon was a lengthy and very labour-intensive process. We know this from the descriptions left in various writings. For example, records tell how in 1374, the King of France ordered his Lieutenant in Lower Normandy to hire the services of a:

> cannoneer to make a certain large cannon throwing stones and fire them as often as might be required at the planned siege of the castle of Sir John Chandos at St. Sauveur le Vicomte.

Muzzle of recreated hoop and stave-construction gun of the serpentine style.

A Barrel is Made for a Cannon *continued*

For his services the cannoneer was to be paid at the rate of fifteen gold pieces per month. The following year, 1375, writings of Jehan le Mercier, a Councillor to the Court of Philip VI of France records the events surrounding the building of a barrel for a cannon using the hoop and stave method. He tells how he was instructed to organize the manufacture of *un grand canon de fer* (a large cannon of iron). It is a most informative document and is probably one of the earliest sources to provide an insight into how cannon barrels of the period were built. He tells how the work was directed by the *maistre des canons*, Bernard de

Monferrat, and the production of just one barrel demanded the services of thirteen men comprising: 'three master smiths, one common smith, eight assistants and one labourer'.

They erected three forges, surrounded by a fence to keep onlookers at bay, in the marketplace of the town of Caen, in the Normandy Region of France. They set to work in early March and completed the work by 3 May, having rested each Sunday and observed a day's holiday on 23 April. For the process the workforce used some 2,110lb (945kg) of iron and 200lb (90kg) of steel. Mercier's writings tell how the

Wrought iron English hoop and stave barrel built in the fifteenth century. It was to be the main design for producing larger calibre weapons until casting techniques improved.

English fifteenth-century bombard made from the 'hoop and stave' method of construction. It had a slow rate of fire and much energy would have been lost as the powder blasted from around the ill-fitting projectile. Nevertheless, it would have produced the desired result and inflicted damage on the target and great injuries on the defenders.

A Barrel is Made for a Cannon *continued*

barrel of the weapon was built up using longitudinal bars of iron, which had been forged into shape and then welded together using heat and hammering. Hooped bands of wrought iron were then heated and fitted over the cylinder to secure the bars in place. After this it was wrapped with some 90lb (40kg) of rope which was tightly bound, and on top of this were stitched leather hides. This latter covering was sometimes greased in order to protect the barrel from the weathering elements of rain and thus reduce the onset of corrosion.

Finally the barrel was set on a specially constructed wooden framework and loaded for test firing, at least twice, using stone shot. Having been proved on 5 May it was then transported 56 miles (90km) west to take part in siege of the castle at St. Sauveur de Vicomte.

To put this process into perspective, this work was conducted at a time when iron cost 5 pence per kilo and lead cost 10 pence per kilo, which puts the cost of raw materials for manufacturing this one cannon at £50. That is to say approximately £2,500 in modern terms, without any other costs being taken into consideration, such as labour, charcoal for the forges or the leather covering and rope or even the carriage made for its transportation. One can see from these prices that only the very richest nobles such as dukes, kings and princes could afford to have such weapons manufactured. Indeed, it could be said that it was this which led to the downfall of the knight and ultimately the end of the feudal system.

Large fifteenth-century English bombard. It is muzzle loaded and constructed by the hoop and stave method.

DIFFERENT TYPES OF ARTILLERY PIECES

Artillery pieces were now beginning to be called different names to distinguish the size and type of gun. Some of these were mythical beasts and others carried names of real animals such as falcon, saker and shrimp. In England, for example, there were bombards, salcons, sakers, culverins and basilisks (named after a mythical serpent which legend had could kill with a glance). Basilisk may also come from the Spanish term *pasavolante* meaning 'fast action'. In the Burgundian Army the artillery train contained weapons called veuglaries, to be used in sieges, which had a barrel length in the order of 2.54m (8.3ft) with a bore between 500mm ($19^1/_2$in) and 250mm ($9^3/_4$in). An example of this type of weapon, mounted on a wooden frame with a pair of solid wooden wheels, is still to

Recreated fifteenth-century gunner. He wears a leather apron to prevent powder from contaminating his clothing and causing a potentially lethal accident. He is loading the pots in readiness for inserting them into the chamber of the gun. This method improved the rate of fire and made it more deadly.

be found in the display of artillery at Castelnaud, in the Perigord Region of France. The Burgundian artillery train also contained cast bronze weapons such as breech-loading bombards and coulverines (perhaps a corruption of the Latin term *colubra* meaning serpent). The weapon design known as coulverin, or 'snake', is believed to have been developed in Germany during the fourteenth century and was defined by its long barrel. Another similar type of cannon was termed the 'serpentine' and was in effect a larger version of the coulverine.

The types of ammunition fired by these

Barrel of a weapon known as a veuglaire on display at Castlenaud in Dordogne, France. Comparable versions were in use across Europe with many armies.

Recreated falconet showing a small style of the field piece. It was useful at close quarters and popular in use across Europe. It was light enough to be mounted in various roles, including use onboard ships.

weapons could be either stone, shaped into round balls by stonemasons, or dart-like projectiles, the shafts of which had leather wound around them to make them fit the barrel of the cannon. The dart projectiles were not well suited to warfare, but they were still fired at buildings such as the castle of Rihoult in Artois, perhaps in the vain hope of hitting an individual, to which purpose such projectiles were better suited. Very small pieces were sometimes referred to as 'minions', possibly a corruption of the French word *mignon*, to mean something very small. This type of artillery piece would

Range of historical styles of early gunpowder artillery, including a barrel for a swivel gun, robinet and a veuglaire.

remain in usage until well into the seventeenth century where it was used to fire a cannon ball weighing 2kg ($4^1/_2$lb), using 1.5kg ($3^1/_4$lb) of powder, out to a range stated as being '1400 paces'. But it was the large balls which were used with greater effect in siege operations. Between 1382 and 1388 the Keeper of the Privy Wardrobe to Richard II, Ralph de Halton, is known to have purchased seventy-three cannons from a gun founder called William Woodward. At least forty-seven of these weapons weighed 380lb (170kg). Later records, dated from 1399, for the Tower of London which list 'artillery and other things' states that 408 springald arrows fletched with tin and forty-four cannon of bronze and iron were held there. Unfortunately no sizes are given for these pieces. Names of individual pieces of artillery would also appear on the lists of clerks from the early part of the fifteenth century, and continue to show that there were still many non-standard cannons 'lying about the Tower [of London]'. According to one such item the term 'bastard' was being applied to any piece which did not properly fall into a category. For example, one such weapon is recorded in 1475 as being a 'great bastard gun and her chamber, called the Messenger'. It shows how proper name terms were being applied in an affectionate manner to artillery pieces, almost as a way of identifying the weapon as being familiar to anyone who may have encountered it before.

Smaller Scale Artillery Pieces

However, not all individual pieces of artillery were built to the large scale. In 1382, it is recorded how the army of Ghent moved against the forces of Bruges and in their train they had a number of particular weapons termed ribauldequins. These were muzzle-loading cannons of small calibre mounted on light wheeled carts and are first mentioned in a list of accounts from the City of Bruges as early as 1339. In the following year at least one is known to have been used in guarding the gate at Tournay. The ribauldequin was a popular weapon and in widespread use, and was referred to variously as ribaude, ribaudequin, ribaudekin or ribaldi. But whatever the term, the design was recognizable from a number of barrels, frequently as many as seven, being grouped together on a wooden base, and mounted on a wheeled carriage. It was quite an advanced design for the period, and on firing either a single barrel or a whole volley could be discharged. This particular weapon can be seen as being the first real weapon which would later be termed as 'field artillery'. The name ribauldequin, or its variant, is believed to be derived from the wheeled carriage on which the barrels were mounted.

One particular version of the ribauldequin was that fielded by Antonio della Scala, the Lord of Verona in Northern Italy, who is known to have had three large weapons of this type constructed, each of which comprised 144 barrels. The barrels were mounted in three tiers of forty-eight barrels, with each tier divided into four sections each with twelve barrels. Each is believed to have stood some 20ft (6m) in height, pulled by four horses and fired by three men. Inevitably, it proved to be too cumbersome for use on the battlefield. Other, more conventional, models of ribauldequin were pulled by draught animals to the site of battle where they were manhandled into position by the crew. This allowed better mobility on the battlefield than the large bombard range of weapons which it frequently supported during siege operations. The multiple barrel design could provide fire support to

Recreated triple barrel ribauldequin on two-wheeled carriage. This was a close-quarters weapon and inflicted great injuries on men and horses.

Recreated triple barrel ribauldequin. Some had many more barrels than this modern reproduction, and some could fire single barrels or in ripple-effect blasts.

the heavier artillery's slow rate of fire and engage defenders moving about the walls.

In 1389 the Veronese dispatched these massive ribauldequins to fight the Paduan forces at the Battle of Castagno. Unfortunately for della Scala's forces their secret weapons became stuck in boggy ground and never reached the field of battle, resulting in a victory for the Paduans. Some accounts describe designs of ribauldequins which could be stripped down to permit each barrel to be carried by one man. When they came to be used in battle these could either be re-assembled on the wheeled cart or fired by each man as an individual weapon. Some now believe that this may be the origin of weapons that would go on to become the hakbuchse or hackbut and arquebuses in later years. There are surviving examples of smaller ribauldequin to be found in artillery museums around the world. One such is a very fine twelve-barrelled design, which could fire its barrels in volleys of three, and is to be seen in the castle of Castelnaud, in the Perigord Region of France, where it is shown mounted on a wheeled-carriage.

DEVELOPMENTS IN MANUFACTURE

As is often the case when new technology appears, either military or civilian, bigger, better and more effective models are demanded. And so it was with the new development of artillery. When traditional metallurgical methods of casting the *pots de fer* could not meet the demand for bigger weapons, new methods of manufacturing had to be adapted to keep pace with supply and demand. And so it was that various methods, including the utilization of the coopers' skills, were adapted over the years. It has been calculated that within fifteen years of the first illustrations of *pots de fer* appearing, which were castings of one piece, more complicated designs cast in two sections were being manufactured.

As metallurgy advanced, not only did the manufacturing techniques of the guns change, but so

too did the projectiles used, which finally moved away from stone balls to cast-iron balls. The first weapons had been used to fire projectiles made variously from lead, iron and stone. Metal was obviously an expensive commodity and the trend in projectiles moved towards stone balls. However, as the fourteenth century progressed, so the trend went in full circle and once more came back to the use of iron as projectiles. The move is believed to have been started in Italy and by 1400 iron balls were in almost universal use. They were proven to have more destructive power against targets constructed from masonry, and size-for-size iron balls were heavier than stone shot. Not only were they easier to produce, but any iron balls fired by an enemy could be melted and recast for use once more. Furthermore, casting methods had advanced to a stage where balls of a consistent size could be made, which would fit the barrel more accurately.

Another advance was the innovation of mounting the weapons on wheeled carriages. This permitted them to be moved by horses or oxen in order to keep pace with an army on the march, albeit very slowly.

EFFECTIVE USE OF ARTILLERY

The increase in demand for artillery led to the weapons being refined and developed, so that by 1377 the Duke of Burgundy had one of the most powerful artillery trains in Europe. In fact, the chronicler Froissart writes how the Burgundian artillery numbered 140 weapons, some of which were capable of firing round stone projectiles weighing over 200lb (90kg), which equates to a calibre of about 16.5in (420mm), and are recorded as having been used at the siege of Odruik in the same year. So successful was the Burgundian artillery at this action that the walls of the castle were breached by the stone balls, thereby forcing the surrender of the English commander of the castle, William de Weston. On conclusion of this action, the Duke of Burgundy then ordered larger weapons capable of firing stone balls with calibres of at least 21in (530mm) and weighing 450lb (200kg). Only two years earlier, in 1375, Owen of Wales was on the receiving end of such an artillery bombardment during the siege of the castle of St. Sauveur-le-Vicomte on the Normandy coast in France. At one point, the French deployed at least forty pieces of gunpowder artillery which directed their fire to batter the walls of the castle. They are known to have used both iron and stone projectiles which, for the first time, produced a notable effect. Although the walls were not breached, the fire from these pieces harassed the defenders to such a degree that they could not offer resistance. As the chronicles of the time record 'They were so covered by the engines that they dare not go into the town or outside the castle but stayed in the towers.'

One projectile which did penetrate the walls is reported to have entered a room in which a sick English knight lay in bed and made a noise 'as if the thunder itself had entered his chamber' as the heavy ball rolled around the interior. No longer were castles and walled towns secure from the battering effect of iron cannon balls, which could smash through these structures more effectively than stone projectiles.

Very large guns (bombards) are shown in the illustrated manuscripts of the period, such as the Chronicles of Friossart and the Beauchamp Chronicles, where they are depicted as being used against castles and towns during siege operations. Even allowing for the fact that the artist does not portray these devices to scale or with any great attention to detail, they are probably representative of the type

Recreated fifteenth-century gunners loading their weapon which is of the serpentine style. Long wooden-handled tools for loading are being used in a manner which is believed to be representative of the time.

Recreated fifteenth century gunners loading a serpentine-style weapon in the manner which is representative of the period.

of artillery in use at the time. These 'terrifying engines' held a fascination for illustrators of the period and even in 1450 were still being recorded in works such as *Chronique d'Angleterre*. The accuracy of these guns during their period of emergence can only be guessed at, but when used against targets the size of a town or castle they must have been impressive. Such targets did not move and any hit would have counted as producing effective results. There are few accounts telling of the effectiveness of such artillery against troops in the open. Obviously casualties were inflicted by such weapons and a large stone ball would have killed or maimed anyone careless enough to remain in its path. Such projectiles would have caused severe crushing injuries, and even if not immediately fatal, shock or secondary infection would be likely to kill the victim at a later stage.

GUNPOWDER

In the fourteenth century gunpowder comprised a mixture of three constituent compounds, which at the time could be blended in varying percentages. The basic mixture comprised of 41 per cent saltpetre, 30 per cent sulphur and 29 per cent charcoal. Over centuries these percentages would vary greatly and certainly each country had its own preferred mixture for gunpowder. Even during the time of the Napoleonic Wars in the first part of the nineteenth century, there was much discrepancy concerning the proportions of these compounds required to produce the best quality gunpowder. Today the formula for gunpowder is still based on these three ingredients but has been standardized as 75 per cent saltpetre, 10 per cent sulphur and 15 per cent charcoal. In the early days, the main

Illustration from a medieval manuscript showing serpentines in use, c. 1470. Note the shape of the gun carriages, which resemble the shafts of a hand cart, which would have made manoeuvring and transporting easier than with large weapons.

drawback to gunpowder was the fact that it had a tendency to separate down into its compounds, according to size of the granular compounds, through the effects of vibration during transportation. This phenomenon produced poor burning rates, and even complete failure to ignite, when it came to be used on the battlefield. One way of overcoming the separation action was to mix the three compounds on the battlefield just before required. This was an extremely dangerous task, because even the slightest spark or lack of concentration could result in spontaneous combustion. This hazard had been recognized early on by Roger Bacon, when he instructed that the mixture should only be blended on a marble surface which was smooth and free of all abrasive surfaces. As techniques in powder handling advanced so too did the method by which it was blended. Later manufacturing methods, developed in France in the fifteenth century, would lead to gunpowder being mixed as a coarse paste, dried and then very care-

fully 'milled' or 'corned' to produce grains which could be sifted to give powder that could be used in different applications. This included very fine powder for priming the vent or touch hole when preparing to fire. These advances meant that gunpowder did not separate down when transported, although handling gunpowder on the battlefield would always be a high risk activity because the men serving the guns had to have a fire constantly burning to provide a source from which to ignite the powder. This was an ever-present threat and was no doubt responsible for many accidents.

One of the first significant names to emerge in the manufacture of gunpowder during the fourteenth century was Merckel Gast of Frankfurt am Main. It was towards the end of this period that his obviously advanced means of handling gunpowder thrust him into pre-eminence. Various accounts record how Gast was credited with the ability to manufacture gunpowder reputed to last in storage for sixty years. This was obviously an apocryphal story related to promote the man's talents, because no one in their right mind would have stored gunpowder for that long without using it. He is believed to have produced the longevity of the powder he mixed by using compounds which only Gast knew and had personally refined himself. He is also understood to have been capable of restoring the explosive properties of powder which had been 'spoiled', presumably by moisture or settling during transportation. Gast was obviously a master in his trade because he is known to have had a deep understanding on all aspects of artillery and the emerging handguns of the time. He was also reputed to have been capable of casting the barrels of cannons and to understand how to site them for greatest effect before battle.

DEFENSIVE FORTIFICATIONS

In response to the appearance of gunpowder artillery, fortifications had to evolve if the castle was to survive an attack by an enemy using cannons. And so it was that the first true arms race began as first one side, and then the other, developed bigger and more powerful guns and deployed them in ever greater numbers. In the pre-gunpowder age, castle builders had responded to their masters' calls to make their castles stronger by simply building the walls as high and as thick as possible in order to prevent scaling by troops using climbing aids. Whilst this was a good counter against equipment such as ladders and battering rams, it meant that the walls now became prime targets. Indeed, the first bombards showed just how vulnerable walls of castles were to artillery and that they could be defeated by cannons during a siege operation. To illustrate this point, it has been calculated that, in order for a medieval battering ram to produce the same damage as a cannon ball weighing 36lb (16kg) fired at close range, the battering ram would have had to weigh 40,000lb (18,200kg) and require the efforts of some 1,000 men.

The castle builders quickly realized that they

had to incorporate special positions into their defensive fortification plans from which cannons could fire. One of the first castles in England to incorporate such firing positions was Bodiam, completed in 1390, where the walls have been pierced just a few feet above ground level and the gatehouse was also adapted to incorporate firing positions. Cities, too, were also beginning to adapt their defences to diminish the effects of cannon fire and incorporate cannons to retaliate against attackers. In 1369 records from the register of accounts for Arras, in Belgium, note how the gates of the town were protected by cannon, twelve arrows and a supply of powder. In England, the city port of Southampton, which had been attacked by French artillery in 1338, was by 1386 defended by sixty large bore cannons, one of which had a calibre of 50cm (20in). The city of Canterbury, in Kent, redesigned its defences between 1375 and 1381 so that it could incorporate at least twenty specially constructed gunports. However, in England this reaction to artillery was not widespread and at first only those castles and cities in the south of England, deemed to be most at risk from French attack, were adapted to incorporate cannons in their defences and strengthen their walls to withstand bombardment. But as England withdrew from France, internal wars, such as the Wars of the Roses, would divide England so these countermeasures to artillery spread to other parts of the country. Other European countries were also beginning to learn that castles were vulnerable to cannon fire and were accordingly re-modelled and strengthened to meet this new threat.

TERMINOLOGY

As the fourteenth century closed, a range of names were applied to distinguish various types of artillery pieces, including birds, reptiles and other strange terms. Some were obviously applied to designate certain sizes of weapons, but in view of the fact that most gunpowder weapons at this time would have been made as individual pieces, lacking a standard calibre, they were more likely built after a style. Some weapons were given proper names by the men who operated them in order to identify individual weapons. The range of weapons referred to as culverins is understood to have been named after a mythical serpent which spat fire and smoke. They were divided into whole culverin and demi-culverin, which fired projectiles of 18lb (8kg) and 9lb (4kg) in weight respectively.

The term calibre, which distinguishes the size of a projectile, is in itself very interesting. The

Bonaguil Castle, Dordogne, France. Early medieval castle modified to take gunpowder artillery.

word is believed to originate from an Arabic word *calib* which means model. From this expression and others, we can build up a picture of how many different countries and cultures all contributed their influence on the development of artillery. Names of other weapons included, for example, the small falconet, which, depending on the actual gun founder, could fire a projectile between 1lb (0.5kg) and 3lb (1.4kg) in weight. The syren fired a ball weighing 60lb (27kg) and the basilisk fired a ball of 48lb (22kg). Other weapons, along with their weight of shot, included: cannon royal (sometimes called carthoun) 48lb (22kg); bastard cannon ($^3/_4$ carthoun) 36lb (16kg); half-carthoun 24lb (11kg); saker 5lb (2.3kg) to 8lb (3.6kg); dragon 6lb (2.7kg); serpentine 4lb (1.8kg).

AT THE END OF THE CENTURY

Despite the widespread use and acceptance of gunpowder weapons on the battlefield during the fourteenth century the actual artillery revolution did not spread with the rapidity that one might have imagined. Although it had become well established during this time, it would not be until the mid-fifteenth century, at engagements such as the Battle of Castillon in 1453, that it would become

Medieval castle at Tarascon in Provence, France, showing the tall vertical walls which were an ideal target for artillery. The castle has been fired on and signs are evident on the walls.

Mont Orgueil castle on Jersey in the Channel Islands. Modified to take gunpowder artillery in the fifteenth century.

the instrument with which to win battles. It was there, at the last major battle in the final year of the seemingly endless Hundred Years War, that the French utilized their cannons to great effect and inflicted such a defeat on the English that it drove them out of France and led to a conclusive end to more than 100 years of intermittent fighting. The fifteenth century saw the establishment of *companies d'ordonnance* in France which in turn led to other European countries founding standing armies, the emergence of professional soldiers and the end of feudalism. All the time the use of artillery was increasing and gradually spread across western Europe where, ironically, it created more of an impact on warfare than in the Far East

where gunpowder is believed to have first been discovered.

As the fourteenth century came to a close, an unknown chronicler of the period recorded:

Hardly a man and bravery in matters of war are of use any longer because guile, betrayal, treachery together with the gruesome artillery pieces have taken over so much that fencing, fighting, hitting and armour, weapons, physical strength or courage are not of much use any more. Because it happens often and frequently that a virile brave hero is killed by some forsaken knave with a gun ...

A recreated weapon of the type known as a serpentine. It shows the wooden handled tools for loading. It is breech loading and has wheels for mobility, which was a turning point in artillery design for the battlefield. Note the crude, but effective means of elevating the barrel, which used the vertical bar on top of which is a gunner's helmet.

Recreated fifteenth-century weapon of the style termed as a falconet. As a field piece, it was best used against infantry and cavalry. However, after the opening bombardments they had to suspend firing as the battle usually developed in front of their firing position.

Types of artillery weapons termed sakers in action during an engagement of the fifteenth century. They are a field piece and became popular across Europe.

3   Artillery Rises to Prominence: 1400 to 1500

By the beginning of the fifteenth century, gunpowder artillery had been used in some parts of Europe for more than eighty years. By this stage there was hardly a credible European army which did not have some form of this weaponry which it could deploy on the battlefield. The types of weapons still varied greatly, as did their overall size and the weight of the projectile they could fire. The actual number of gunpowder weapons which an army could deploy also varied from one country to another. One thing was certain at this point, if an army did not possess even a few gunpowder weapons it would be at a disadvantage compared to an adversary that did possess such weaponry. Countries and states, such as France and Burgundy, would continue their rise to greatness through the power of their artillery. Emergent countries, such as Turkey, would also make their presence felt through the strength of their artillery. Fighting of the Hundred Years War between France and England was still continuing and other wars between rival states and factions would see the use of artillery spread. Voyages of discovery would also carry artillery to continents where such powerful weapons had never been imagined. This would allow European states to establish overseas empires, and bring huge wealth to countries such as Spain.

DEVELOPMENTS

The direct development of artillery in the fifteenth century was to be marked by three major improvements. Firstly was the introduction of an improved technique in gunpowder manufacture, known as 'milling' or 'corning', which made it less likely for the gunpowder to separate. However, there was a drawback to using this type of gunpowder which was more powerful than the early compounds. The amount of gaseous pressures built up by this powder when fired was so great that it caused some of the older style barrels to burst, especially those which had been built using the hoop and stave method of construction. This in itself meant that those armies still equipped with older weapons were initially prevented from fully accepting it until they acquired new weapons.

However, it was the introduction of corned gunpowder which served as a catalyst to greatly speed up the development and introduction into service of cannons fitted with barrels that would not burst when fired with the new powder. This was actually the second improvement of the age. Techniques were developed to permit barrels to be manufactured as a single casting through the use of cast iron, which produced stronger weapons capable of withstanding the pressures developed on firing the new 'corned' powder.

The third factor was the introduction of another type of weapon to augment the range of artillery. This was the mortar, which served alongside standard artillery, but was designed to fire with its barrel set at a high angle of trajectory so as to 'lob' the projectiles over defensive walls. Battlefield tactics were also to change.

Improvements in Gunpowder Manufacture

'Corning' is believed to have been developed in France during the fifteenth century. It was a more

Fifteenth-century mortar on solid wooden bed. It is a basic design not unlike the earliest known image of a gunpowder weapon in the de Millemete chronicles. It would have had a limited range and been of dubious use.

expensive process but it produced better powder and made handling of the substance significantly safer. The process involved mixing the three constituent compounds together in a wet paste, which was then allowed to dry into a flat 'cake'. These 'cakes' could then be milled into corn-like granules which could be sifted out into grades according to the size of the grains. Since such a process allowed regular-sized grains to be produced, the efficiency of the powder was greatly improved because burning rates were constant. But this improved method of manufacturing the gunpowder did not remedy the fact that a lot of the chemical energy released on firing was lost either as propelling gases vented forward around the ill-fitting projectile, known as windage, or as powder blasted from the cannon whilst still burning. These defects were to be partly redressed when

iron projectiles were introduced in place of the roughly hewn stone balls and longer barrelled weapons, which permitted the powder to combust before the cannon ball left the muzzle, were developed.

BOMBARDS

To the east, Turkey had been trading with other eastern Asian countries for hundreds of years and the country is credited with introducing cannons to the continent. Turkey was also trading with some western European states and drawing on their expertise to produce improved artillery. The method of constructing barrels for artillery using the built up method with bundles of iron bars on to which iron hoops were shrunk to secure them, was still in use at the time, and it was these that Turkey exported.

However, the new casting techniques were improving to the point where gunsmiths could produce single-piece barrels of quite extraordinary size. These large cannons were still used almost exclusively for siege operations against castles and walled towns, but some were available for the defence of fortifications. These weapons, still referred to as bombards, were moved from one location to another by carts drawn by oxen. In some circumstances they were sited on gun platforms, usually mounds of earth, specially constructed for the duration of the siege. Sometimes these platforms incorporated mountings constructed from logs, which again, had been specially prepared for the purpose. To increase the angle of the barrel in order to increase the range of the projectile, the labour force lifted the forward end of the barrel using pulleys and either piled stones and earth under the barrel or inserted large blocks of wood. Such huge weapons were not suited to

mobile warfare on the battlefield, which meant that once sited they would not be moved. This left them vulnerable to attack should an enemy put in an assault on the gun positions. Their very size meant they would not be easily carried from the battlefield in such an action, and would more likely be rolled from their mountings.

Projectiles

Projectiles at this stage, particularly for the large bombards, were still made from either iron or stone. Even by the fifteenth century, base metals, such as iron, copper and lead were expensive and the use of such materials for cannonballs, especially iron, was still restricted. Even by 1530, it has been calculated that the annual output of iron in western Europe was still only between 100,000 tonnes and 150,000 tonnes, which stretched this resource to its maximum, considering that armour was still being worn, and weapons such as swords and other edged weapons were in common use.

Preparing to fire a recreated bombard on its wooden 'telaria' mounting. This angle would have fired the projectile at a very low trajectory and would have inflicted great injuries on men and horses caught in its path.

The use of stone for projectiles was still widespread and the methods for cutting and shaping stone into cannon balls was well developed in many countries, which employed the services of masons. Indeed, their skills in producing such projectiles were much sought after, but despite their best efforts, demand often outstripped supply. This meant that these hand-cut balls were often sent out in an unfinished state and were a poor fit for the barrels of the cannons. This compounded the problem of windage, an effect caused by the propelling gases from the burning being expelled around the stone ball, which led to the projectile either falling short of the target or not striking it with sufficient energy to inflict any great damage. Some of these balls could have as much as a quarter of an inch gap around their diameter inside the barrel. The slow rate of fire with the bombards and, in some cases, their poor hitting power, meant that defenders could frequently effect repairs to a section of damaged wall before the next shot landed. Another countermeasure used by defenders to reduce the effect of artillery bombardment was to drape large fascines or bundles of wood and wool over parts of walls under attack so as to try and lessen the impact of the huge cannon balls. The accuracy of these weapons was very poor and it would have been unusual for two projectiles to land in even close proximity.

The moment of firing a recreated fifteenth-century bombard. It shows how large clouds of smoke and muzzle blast and flash were created on firing. A lot of the energy was lost due to ill-fitting stone balls, but they could still produce damage on walls and inflict severe injuries and death.

Great clouds of smoke produced on firing a recreated fifteenth-century bombard. This would have choked and blinded all those on the battlefield.

WEAKNESSES

By this period, artillery was either muzzle loaded, which is to say that the whole process of loading the powder and ball was carried out at the front of the cannon using long-handled wooden tools, or breech loading. Bombards deployed at sieges could have been of either design. The breech loaders, which used separate pre-loaded pots, could produce faster rates of firing, but still required the skill and care of several men to operate them properly. Barrels, whether of cast iron or built-up, were notoriously prone to exploding unexpectedly when they were fired. As the barrel ruptured and tore itself apart the crew could be maimed or even killed in the resulting explosion. The reason for this phenomenon lay in the fact that cast-iron barrels may have had inherent weaknesses caused either by hairline fractures, which were faults present during manufacture, or by pockets of air trapped during the casting process. With the bar-

rels made in the stackened method of hoops and staves, weaknesses were caused by the individual longitudinal bars becoming separated and splitting apart during firing. If detected in time, the men serving the cannon would attempt to repair the fault by simply pouring molten metal, often no more than lead, into these fractures in order to seal the barrel of the cannon.

There were many other ways in which firing accidents could be caused. One of these was a lack of adequate sealing at the breech, on those weapons where a separate firing chamber was used. This is known as 'obturation' by modern artillerymen, but in the fifteenth century this term was unknown. Escaping gases were under great pressure and could inflict serious injury if a man were unwitting enough to be standing too close. No wonder, then, that to inspire courage and steadfastness gunners soon adopted the figure of St. Barbara, the patron saint of thunder and lightning, as their personal guardian. In 1417 the cannoneers

Detail of breech of a fifteenth-century English bombard. It clearly shows the touch hole, through which the main charge of propellant powder in the chamber would have been ignited.

the projectile to increase accuracy and stability of the projectile when fired. Although this was another effect unknown to gunners of the time, some evidence has been uncovered which reveals that early attempts at rifling may have been conducted in Germany towards the end of the fifteenth century. Other experiments into barrel design were taking place in Germany, which included trying to produce a multiple-barrel weapon. One of these is shown in an illustration which depicts eight barrels mounted on a turntable. Another similar artillery piece appears in the manuscript Codex Germanicus 600, held in the Staatsbibliothek, Munich, and shows four barrels mounted on a turntable set at 90 degree angles to one another. It is believed that the barrels in each case would be loaded and rotated into action for firing, thereby providing a number of shots in quick succession. A different type of multi-barrelled weapon also developed in Germany, around 1450, was the Orgelgeschutze, which one writer of the period described as 'organ-pipes placed upon a broad carriage'. One surviving example shows five barrels of small calibre, enclosed by a wooden casing, and would appear to be a variation on the ribaudekin, which was still in use. Although such experimentation into artillery was being conducted during this period, the real art and craft of designing weapons, their manufacturing and employment was being passed down by word of mouth from gunsmith to apprentice as they worked. This meant the circle of the initiated was intentionally kept small and knowledge was acquired only through hands-on practice. However, by the end of the century this would change when the first specially prepared books on the subject were published.

The exact strength of the barrels of cannons was always the great unknown factor. Some barrels were built with undetected faults which remained invisible until they exploded with a final suddenness. On the other hand some barrels became progressively weakened through use that they eventually reached a point where the barrel could no longer resist the great internal pressure and it self-destructed with terrible consequences to the

at Lille declared themselves to be 'confrères de Sainte Barbe' after they had adopted her as their patron saint. In fact the Spanish term 'santabarbara' means a depository for explosives and on French ships the powder room was called a 'Sainte Barbe'.

The weaknesses in barrel manufacture led to some designs of weapons becoming unpopular. The barrels of all artillery at this time were smoothbore, which is to say they lacked the internal grooves which would have imparted spin on men serving the weapon. This fundamental weakness had been realized by gun founders for some time, but a solution to the problem was something that continued to elude them. One method used to test the strength of a barrel was to simply load and fire it with ever increasing charges until a point was reached where it was firing to greater tolerances than the gun founder believed it could withstand. If it survived this very basic, virtually unscientific test, it was passed as being suitable for normal service. This method of proving the barrel is recorded as being in use in 1375 at the city of Basle, where it is stated that an area outside the walls had been laid aside for the purposes of proving and testing guns in such a manner. This method of proving to the point of destruction was widely used, and in England cannons subjected to such trials were considered to be 'weak, broken, noisom, used up and broken and wasted in trials and assay'. It was vital that cannons were tested, because their failure in time of battle could mean the difference between failure and victory. Those cannons that had been subjected to the test were indicated as having passed successfully by being stamped with the embossed mark on the barrels. This was usually a recognized crest relating to the proving authority or the coat of arms of the town where the barrel had been cast and tested. It is very likely that there existed some proving bodies which were less than scrupulous in their task and merely examined the barrels by sight, foregoing the trouble of a full scientific examination.

Some barrels exploded during use, as evident with this sixteenth-century English bronze barrel. Exactly when this occurred is not known, but the force of the explosion shows how dangerous it would have been to the gun crew.

THE EMERGENCE OF REFERENCE WORKS

As the fifteenth century progressed so too did the skill of the artillerymen and the quality of the cannons themselves. By 1420 the first written works covering the workings of gunpowder artillery and casting of barrels for cannons were beginning to be circulated. These were hand printed, and for the most part would not be widely available as reference works until more than 100 years later. One outstanding book of this time was a German Firework Book, in which it is explained how a master smith should be a:

thoughtful employer, and should be able to make all the chemical products appropriate to his craft, as well as firedarts, fireballs and other pyrotechnic devices that could be used to kill or deter an enemy.

It would have been obvious to most military minds of the time that the subject of artillery was progressing at such a rate that it was becoming too complicated for a single man to commit to memory. Reference books would be the only way of alleviating the problem and over the coming years more works on the subject would appear. The master gunner would probably not only had to be highly proficient in battlefield skills, but also well

An attempt to produce a two-barrelled weapon with barrels set at an improbable 90 degrees to one another. Needless to say, it was not developed.

Early sixteenth-century illustration showing a design with eight barrels mounted on a turntable to increase rate of firing. A very fanciful notion, it did not progress much further than the drawing board.

A single barrel of an artillery piece mounted on a turntable to give a full 360 degrees traverse to produce all-round arc of fire. Beyond this artist's concept there does not appear to be much more to this design. Had it been applied to a weapon carried on board a ship, it would have been centuries ahead of its time.

versed in the mathematics required for carrying out calculations and able to read and write for purposes of communication.

Johann Gutenberg is credited with devising mechanical printing in about 1450, an invention which has been called 'the fundamental medium

for a sudden prolific dissemination of knowledge'. Within five years, printing from movable type was invented in Germany, increasing the availability and range of books covering the subject of gunnery. Printed books would continue to be of great importance for gunners because they provided a series of reference works on the complicated and ever-changing gunner's art and allowed the transference of military ideas and thoughts which would, in turn, lead to a cross-fertilization of ideas. Such works in the fifteenth century would go on to include those written by Valturius in 1472, Pliny in 1476 and Frontinus in 1480.

There was little, if any, education outside of the noble classes, which meant that few people had sufficient education to read, let alone grasp the fundamental mathematical skills required of competent gunners. Those individuals experienced in the technicalities of artillery were in great demand, and offered handsome inducements to enter the direct employment of kings and dukes and also by cities and states. It seems safe to assume that one of the more inquisitive figures who read the books on artillery was Leonardo da Vinci, 1452–1519. With his enquiring mind and scientific interests it is quite possible that he would have read and understood the topics being described. In fact, in his own *Codex Atlanticus*, da Vinci claims to have a working knowledge of the art of war. In these writings he sets out plans, some of which he may have acquired from other sources, as well as his own original ideas. He would probably have been aware of the types of artillery deployed by Mehomet II at the Siege of Constantinople in 1453 since, although he was only one year old when this event happened, he may well have read accounts of the battle. The Turkish siege of Rhodes in 1480 is something he would probably have heard direct from chroniclers within only weeks or months of the event. Admittedly da Vinci did produce some rather fanciful designs for weapons, but so too did some military thinkers who postulated their own ideas, some of which included the use of horses to push a cart in front of them. One particular impression shows horses pushing a wheeled cart, on

Illustration showing fifteenth-century Austrian artillery. To the left of the picture is a mortar, which was just beginning to be used in conjunction with other forms of artillery.

which is mounted a number of barrels, which have been identified as being ribaldequins. One has to conclude that in this case the artist had probably never seen artillery at first hand and certainly never seen it being moved by horses. Such fanciful illustrations can be dismissed in an instant as being pure fantasy, because a horse can no more push a cart than a sailor can push rope. However, more practical works would go on to ensure the spread of the art and practices of gunnery and its workings, which could only improve as the science of artillery became better understood.

BOMBARDIERS

As early as the turn of the fourteenth into the fifteenth century those men forming the crew of a cannon were beginning to be referred to as

bombardiers, a term which is derived from the Latin *bombus*, to mean a muffled sound. It is interesting to note that Bombardier is an expression still used in the artillery branch of many armies around the world today. In fact, it is actually a recognized term of rank to signify a non-commissioned officer in the Royal Regiment of Artillery in the British Army. By the fifteenth century some European countries were beginning to refer to the men serving in the artillery service by special titles. One of the first was France, where as early as 1411 the term *cannoniers* was being used to identify such men. This expression was seized on by other countries and adopted for military parlance. Such men were, in effect, the master gunners of their day. Another expression to emerge was a Dutch nautical term *matross,* to mean sailor or sailor's mate. This term was expanded to include the labourers in service with artillery crews.

Illustration showing bombards and mortars of c. 1480. The gun carriage is again of the style of shafts fitted to handcarts, while the mortar still lacks the elevating mechanism.

ARTILLERY AT SEA

Ships were now carrying pieces of artillery on a regular basis for their own defence and also for firing at coastal targets. These weapons were simply adaptations of artillery in service with armies and were often secured to fixtures on the ship's deck. An indenture dating from 1411, during the reign of Henry IV of England, gives an indication of the types of weaponry carried by two ships of the

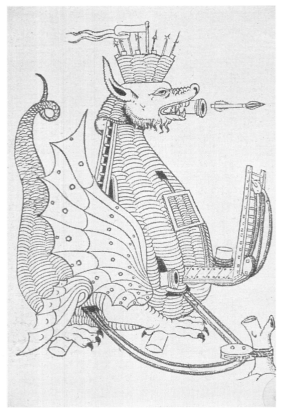

Had this rather fabulous concept been built, it would probably have been blown apart by muzzle blast and recoil when fired.

period; the *Bernard de la Tour* and the *Christopher de la Tour*. The *Bernard* is known to have been equipped with three iron cannons, one of which had a separate chamber, and one brass cannon. The *Christopher*, according to the indenture, was equipped with 'iii cannons de ferr ove v. chambers, un handgonne ... un petit barrel de gonpouder, le quart plein', which puts her armed in a comparable fashion to her sister ship, the *Bernard*. Ships had been carrying artillery as part of their complement since the 1380s and possibly even earlier. Moorish galleys are known to have carried artillery for use against the Tunisian coast and Venetian ships are recorded as having fired on Genoese ships in 1377. However, although these weapons were now at sea,

they would not be used decisively until the Battle of Prevesa in 1538.

THE BURGUNDIAN ARTILLERY

During this century the Dukes of Burgundy, Philip the Good and later his son, Charles the Bold, formerly the Count of Charolais and also known as Charles le Temeraire, were among the first military leaders to incorporate an artillery branch within the structure of their army. Another of their innovative moves was to appoint noblemen as *maitres d'artillerie*. This might be considered as creating an elitist unit, but there was a perfectly logical reason behind this move. The Dukes realized that a man of such standing and high office would have received a better education than an ordinary man-at-arms, and thus his comprehension into the workings of the new weapons of war would be much greater. An added benefit would have been that the man's noble rank would also have made him a natural figure of authority. Another move to improve the use of artillery came when the Dukes developed the tactic of grouping all their cannons together, in order to increase their firepower and effectiveness against the enemy. This replaced the practice of placing individual weapons at various locations around the battlefield with little or no regard to tactical advantages. They had set another precedent and other countries followed the trend. In future, artillery would be assembled into batteries to deliver crushing blows as the effect of their fire was multiplied. The Burgundians were to prove their superiority in artillery many times against various enemies. One of these was the Swiss, who formed mercenary groups from the cantons in their own country. During the fourteenth century the Swiss had dominated the battlefields of northern Italy and Burgundy but their refusal to heed the power of artillery would lead to their downfall. Tactics were changing and emergent weapons such as infantry firearms in the form of arquebuses and artillery were ignored.

The Burgundian artillery train contained a

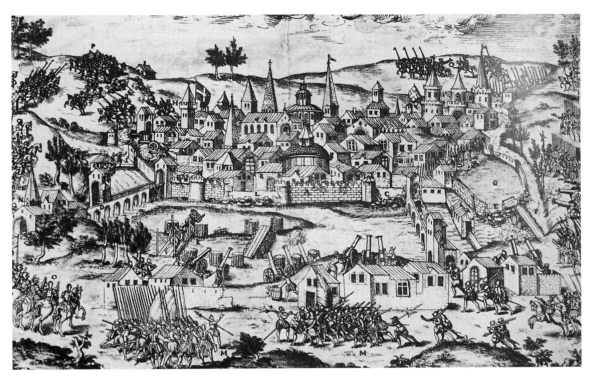

Above   *Illustration showing all arms being used in combination on the battlefield. This shows arqubusiers, with early muskets, pike blocks and artillery.*

Massed ranks of fifteenth-century artillery. A very neat representation showing lighter weapons and a large bombard in the foreground. Such a tidy battlefield with well-coordinated troops and weapons is an idealized impression by the artist.

weapon known as the 'Dulle Griete', possibly taken from the old English to mean 'Muffled Greeting', but was also referred to by the familiar name of 'Mad Margaret'. Believed to have been cast from wrought iron around 1430, this great Bombard of Ghent, measured 18ft (5½m) in length and weighed 15 tons. It fired a stone projectile of 33in (840mm) calibre, approximately 720lb (330kg), using more than 60lb (27kg) of powder. The best gun founders at the time were working in Flanders and manufacturing all manner of pieces of artillery on a regular basis, including one weapon which weighed almost half a ton, with a length of 8ft 6in (2.6m) and a calibre of 4.5in (115mm). Even with their considerable experience in dealing with heavy weapons, the gun founders of Flanders must have found their expertise stretched to the limit with the casting of Dulle Griete.

Another large bombard-type weapon originally made for the Burgundian arsenal was 'Margaret of Mons' or as we know it today 'Mons Meg', which is on display at Edinburgh Castle, Scotland. Smaller than 'Dulle Griete', 'Mons Meg' has a calibre of 19.5in (500mm), is 13ft (4m) in length and weighs 5 tons. With its barrel set at an angle of 45 degrees and loaded with 105lb (48kg) of gunpowder, Mons Meg could fire stone balls weighing 550lb (250kg) or iron balls weighing 1,125lb (510kg) out to ranges of approximately 3,000yd (2,700m) and 1,400yd (1,280m) respectively. It is believed to have built in the Flanders region of Mons, at around 1449 or 1450, for Duke Philip the Good of Burgundy. The weapon was built in two sections, using the 'hoop and stave' method for constructing the barrel, with a cast rear portion forming the powder chamber into which rectangular slots are incorporated in the circumference. This was to permit capstan bars to be inserted in order to unscrew the chamber from the barrel for loading powder and shot. It was then screwed back together and ready for firing. This technique also meant the weapon, sometimes referred to affectionately as 'Munce', could be dismantled for ease of transportation as two smaller loads. This powerful

weapon was presented to James II of Scotland in 1457 as an extravagant gift, however the first official mention of it is not recorded until 1489 when the Lord High Treasurer of Scotland notes in his

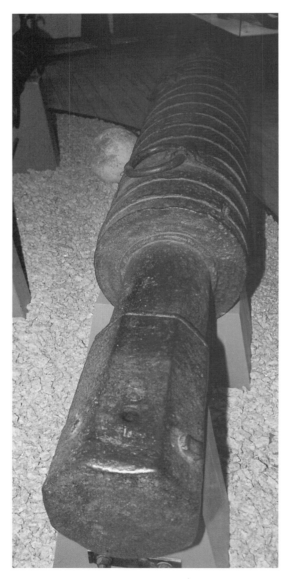

Detail of breech of English fifteenth-century bombard. It shows the touch hole through which the main propellant charge was ignited on firing.

accouts 'ITEM given to the gunners, to drinksilver, when they cartit Monss by the King's command, xviii shillings'. The method of forming the screw joint between the barrel and the powder chamber was very advanced for the day and would have had the added advantage of providing a better gas-tight seal at the breech end.

From these two examples of manufacturing bombards, it can be seen that both methods of constructing barrels were still in common use during the fifteenth century. Gunsmiths of the day clearly understood their trade and were inclined to use whatever methods best suited their means to complete manufacture of a weapon. Examples of these techniques can be seen in many museums today, such as the Royal armouries at Fort Nelson, Fare-

ham, Hampshire, England, where a bombard dating from 1450 forms part of the historical display. This particular weapon could fire stone balls weighing up to 180lb (80kg) and would have been used to attack castle walls during siege operations. The barrel of this particular example is formed from the traditional hoop and stave method, which are tightly stackened, but like Mons Meg the powder chamber is of a single casting or forging. It is believed to have been influenced in design by continental cannons of the period, an opinion that is supported by the fact that Mons Meg was built in Flanders at the time when this particular weapon is dated. The weapon on display has three rings attached to the barrel, which the crew could use to lift it for positioning on its firing blocks.

Recreated fifteenth century bombard, showing how blocks were placed under the front end of the wooden platform or 'telaria', to elevate the barrel. This increased the range and also allowed it to fire with effect against walls of castles.

ADVANCEMENTS IN FRANCE

Undoubtedly the greatest advances in all aspects of artillery in Europe throughout the fifteenth century were made in France. John Keegan, in his book *A History of Warfare*, tells how the French used their artillery to reassert their power over former territories. He writes:

> In 1477 Louis XI of France further extended his area of control over his ancestral lands by using cannon against the castles of the dukes of Burgundy. By 1478, as a result, the French royal house was fully in control of its own territory for the first time since Carolingian days six centuries earlier, and ready to erect a centralised government – supported by a fiscal system in which cannon were the ultimate tax-collectors from refractory vassals.

According to C. Duffy in his book *Siege Warfare*:

> French craftsmen and bell-founder ... by the early 1490s ... had evolved a cannon that was recognisably the same creature that was going to decide battles and sieges for nearly four hundred years to come. The heavy 'built-up' bombard, firing a stone ball from a wooden platform that had laboriously to be lifted onto a cart whenever it changed position, had been replaced by a slender homogeneous bronze-cast tube, no more than eight feet long, its proportions carefully calculated to absorb the progressively diminishing shock of discharge from breech to muzzle. It fired wrought iron balls, heavier than their stone equivalents but, because of that, of three times greater destructive effect for a given bore.

Jean and Gaspard Bureau

French artillery ascendancy started about 1440, and was instituted by the brothers Jean and Gaspard (sometimes spelt Jasper) Bureau. The chronicler Monstrelet wrote of them:

> The king [Charles VII of France] had similarly made provision concerning artillery for his defence and for attacking towns and fortresses. Never in living memory had there been such an assemblage of large bombards, heavy cannon, veuglaires, serpentines, mortars, culverins and ribaudekins and these were amply provisioned with powder, protective coverings known as cats, a great number of carts to transport them, and everything necessary for the capture of towns and castles, and well provided with men to operate them all. They all received their pay daily, and placed under the command of master Jean Bureau, treasurer of France, and Jasper Bureau, master of artillery. These two men endured great dangers and hardships throughout the campaign, for they were attentive to their duty ...

It has been opined that it was they who had the presence of mind to see how best artillery could and should be applied on the battlefield. Indeed, it could be argued that it was their influence that saw the sudden and overwhelming French victories in the closing battles of the Hundred Years War and final defeat of the English. Under their direction the French artillery would batter down the walls of English-held towns and castles with amazing rapidity. Jean Bureau is first heard of during his involvement with the French siege of Meaux in 1439, but his services in the field of artillery had not always been loyal to his French masters. At one time he is known to have served with the English in the role of master of artillery.

One account describes him as being 'a citizen of Paris, a man of small stature but of purpose and daring, particularly skilled and experienced in the use of artillery'. Compared to earlier sieges during the Hundred Years War, those actions conducted by the French during the re-conquest of their territories in Normandy between 1449–1450 were brief affairs.

It seemed that the Bureau brothers were to be found everywhere directing artillery with great enthusiasm. In fact during this time they are credited with having directed at least sixty sieges. Their

Detail of a French fifteenth-century bombard and mortar.

fame spread and the power of their weapons was almost legendary as they provided Charles VII with an 'irresistible' artillery train with which to recover his kingdom. Such was their reputation that some fortresses held by the English simply surrendered once the cannons were in position, especially if they knew the Bureau brothers were in command. Although Jean Bureau was the Treasurer of France, part of the campaign, if not most, was financed by Jacques Coeur, a wealthy and patriotic medieval entrepreneur who supplied a footing of money and credit. At the siege of Harfleur in 1449, for example, a single shot from one of the Bureau brothers' cannons is recorded as passing straight through the ramparts of the castle. At the siege of Bordeaux, conducted between July and October 1453, over a period of ten weeks, Jean Bureau directed an artillery force of some 250 can-

non of various sizes. This force included culverins, long-range cannon of relatively light design, and heavier bombards. Most of the weapons were emplaced for siege operations, but some were sited in order that they might be able to fire over new arcs to cover directions from which an English relief force might approach and thereby repulse them. The action was prosecuted to its fullest and gave the French another victory towards driving the English out of the country. They used artillery in ways never before contemplated, such as at the siege of Cherbourg in April 1450, which was being held by the English. The chronicler Monstrelet records how:

There were even bombards situated on the sea shore between high and low tide, which were weighted with boulders; although they were under water when the tide came in, they were covered with greased skins so that the sea did no harm to their powder, and as soon as the tide went out the cannoneers removed the coverings and continued firing into the town, to the great astonishment of the English, who had never seen anything like it.

Four bombards and one cannon burst while firing at the town …

With such techniques, no wonder the French went on to achieve success in the Hundred Years War.

Casualties and Fatalities

Early gunpowder weapons were far from accurate, and the precise aiming of the weapons was an unknown science.

Stone shot was used extensively until 1500 and its effect on the target was two-fold. On hitting a dwelling such as a house, it would destroy by sheer weight of impact. Any defender in the building was likely to be crushed to death as the building collapsed. However, if the stone shot hit a solid structure, such as a defensive wall, it would probably shatter, thus hurling stone splinters in all directions, inflicting severe injuries on unprotected personnel. Iron balls would not shatter on impact, and were effective as crushing projectiles.

In the open, both types of projectile would have a low trajectory and most likely 'bowl', thus hitting the legs of massed infantry units and smashing limbs. Later projectiles such as the 'grapeshot' and 'canister' were anti-personnel in effect and designed to engage infantry at close quarters like large modern-day shotguns. Further developments included explosive-filled shells which caused buildings to collapse and hurled fragments of metal casing to cause anti-personnel wounds. It was the volume of fire which caused the most damage to buildings and personnel. Only later would accuracy increase the casualty rate and destroy buildings with greater efficiency.

Even though it was impossible accurately to target an individual, the possibility of a key figure being hit could not be entirely dismissed. For example, the English military leader, Lord Salisbury, is recorded as being killed when struck by a single ball at the siege of Orléans on 3 November 1428.

From the gunners' point of view, the early cannons were not entirely failsafe, because of poor metallurgy, and there was always a risk that the weapon could explode on firing. This phenomenon could be caused by an inexperienced gun crew loading their weapon with too great a charge of gunpowder, which led to a build-up of pressure inside the gun, causing the weakened barrel to explode with great force. One such incident occurred in 1408 during the siege of Harlech Castle, Wales, when a bombard called 'The King's Daughter' in the artillery train of Henry V exploded. Another case where the cannon exploded on firing claimed one of the first notable artillery fatalities in the form of James II of Scotland, who was killed at the siege of Roxborough, on 3 August 1460. An account records how 'ane piece of ane misformed gune that brake in the shuting'. Another account of the same incident recalls how:

While this prince, more curious nor became the Majestie of any Kinge, did stand near-hand where the Artylliare was discharged. His thighbone was dung in two by a piece of miss-framed gunne that brake in the shuting, by the which he was stricken to the ground and died hastilie.

When a weapon exploded in this manner, it was no respecter of rank of wealth.

It is interesting to note that in 1415 'The King's Daughter' was again deployed on the battlefield, when it is recorded as being used at the siege of Harfleur between 18 August and 4 October that year. If this is correct, it would seem that gunpowder artillery was so highly prized that even damaged pieces were repaired whenever possible, to allow further use. Whilst 'The King's Daughter' gave better account of itself at this action, inflicting damage on the walls, its rate of fire was so slow that the defenders could repair the damage at night. The town of Harfleur at this time was defended by only 400 French and the walls included twenty-six towers, which were pierced to allow the French defenders to fire their artillery and hand-guns. In fact, an English account of the siege tells how the towers were equipped 'with narrow chinks and places full of holes through which they might annoy us with their tubes, which we in English call "gunnys"'. Henry V is understood to have personally directed the siting of his great siege guns ringing the town of Harfleur, after which he retired to a nearby hill to watch the proceedings. The English maintained their artillery bombardment of the city during the night to deny the defenders any rest. With no sign of a relief force the town was forced to surrender to Henry's forces.

Another early high-placed casualty as a result of cannon fire was John Talbot, Earl of Shrewsbury. He met his death at the Battle of Castillon in 1453 when his horse was struck by a cannon ball. In falling it landed awkwardly and pinned him to the ground where he was dispatched by an ordinary man-at-arms. The exact toll of artillery fire on men-at-arms, such as halbardiers and archers, will probably never be known because their lowly status meant that their losses were never recorded. It should be remembered that longbows, with an accurate range of 200yd (180m), were still in use at this time and all battlefield

casualties were recorded without categorization or classification. The matchlock arquebus may have only been accurate out to 50yd (46m), but it took considerably less time to train a man in its use, which meant that greater numbers of troops, with only rudimentary training, could be armed and quickly put in the field. These weapons would also take a toll on troops in battle, but their effects would not be categorized. Various artillery pieces, such as sakers and medium-sized culverins could, respectively, fire 5lb (2.3kg) and 17lb (7.7kg) projectiles, with some degree of accuracy, out to ranges of 350yd (320m). The maximum range of these weapons was 1,700yd (1,550m) and 2,500yd (2,290m) respectively, which considerably deepened the battlefield and could threaten the baggage trains. This was something that archers could never do and, providing the gunners had sufficient supplies of powder and shot, they could continue to fire almost tirelessly and take steady toll on the opposition.

THE HUNDRED YEARS WAR CONTINUES

By 1415 the countries of France and England had been engaged in the seemingly endless Hundred Years War and had fought one another many times since the beginning in 1337. During the fifteenth century, they were to meet on the battlefield many more times, such as the Battle of Agincourt on 25 October 1415.

In 1413 the regency of England passed to Henry V, who set about forging alliances with Duke John of Burgundy. On 10 August 1415, everything was in place for another assault and Henry set sail for France with an army of 12,000 men. His artillery force is understood to have included at least ten cannons, three of which are reported as being exceptionally large and referred to by such casual names as 'The King's Daughter' and 'London'. His master of engineering was a man by the name of Giles who organized the artillery bombardment of the city of Harfleur, which commenced on 13 August, only three days

after setting out from England. The city of Harfleur was battered badly with the gate and barbican lying in ruins after twenty-seven days of bombardment. On 22 September Master Giles directed that incendiary projectiles be directed against the city and this succeeded in setting fire to wooden structures. There was no great secrecy surrounding incendiary projectiles at this time. An ordinary ball would be coated in tar, which was ignited by the flash of the gunpowder on firing. The English maintained the bombardment and breached the walls. With Harfleur in his hands, Henry had a base from which he could operate. His army had been sorely depleted with sickness and the weather was turning very bad. On 10 October he marched towards the River Somme on his way towards Calais, no doubt hoping to engage the French in battle. His artillery, which had been so successful at the siege of Harfleur, was left behind. No doubt he thought that its weight and the deteriorating conditions of the roads would only hinder his march which was averaging 14 miles (20km) per day. He could not

Recreated fifteenth-century gunner showing how he was lightly equipped apart from his helmet. This was necessary because he worked hard and could not afford to be encumbered by armour.

cross the river because the bridges had either been destroyed or were heavily guarded.

In the end, he managed to find a crossing and the two armies finally came face to face at Agincourt on 25 October 1415. Like its counterpart at Crécy, seventy years earlier, there is contradictory evidence regarding the presence of artillery on the battlefield. We know from records that Henry had left his artillery behind at Harfleur, but records made by the chroniclers who accompanied the

armies on campaign claim that the French had artillery in their lines. Sources vary over this claim and many accounts omit to mention such weapons. However, those which do mention artillery state the weapons were positioned among the French crossbowmen. It is unlikely that the French did have artillery, because, like Henry they would have realized that it would have slowed them down and they would not have kept pace with the English army. In the event, the action was yet another triumph of the English longbowmen over the finest French cavalry. Thus, like the earlier English use of cannons at Crécy in 1345, the effective use of cannons in this battle goes largely unknown. With this victory Henry was safe from further attack and able to march on to Calais without hindrance. He did not linger for very long and departed the country, sailing back to England in November.

In mid-1417 Henry returned to France with his brother Clarence in time to direct the siege of Caen, which at the time was one of the greatest towns in France. Caen had great strategical importance to Henry, because it controlled the entrance to the River Orne, and had to be taken if he was to bring in supplies for his army by sea. In July 1417 Henry commenced the siege which was ably supported by his artillery. Once the town had been encircled by his batteries of artillery, earthworks were thrown up in front of them to protect the gunners. The artillery opened fire on the walls, and by elevating the barrels they were able to fire directly into the town, where the balls impacted to crush buildings and smash equipment. Henry's artillery used incendiary projectiles, which were simply ordinary stone or iron balls coated in tar, to set fire to buildings. The lighter pieces of Henry's artillery were brought closer to the town where they could fire along the gaps between the buildings. The French defenders' artillery was lighter, but had a higher rate of return fire and was far more accurate. However, they could not match the sustained fire of the English artillery which tore great rents in the town's walls which were built in a pre-gunpowder artillery age, and breaches were made at several sites. But, again, artillery did not influence the

Large bombard on display at Castlenaud in Dordogne, France. It has a wooden protective screen around it to shield the gunners from enemy archers and hand-gunners as they loaded the weapon.

outcome. After the town had rejected a number of calls to surrender, Henry assaulted the town from one direction whilst his brother, Clarence, attacked from another approach. The town was entered and, under the articles of war of the day when a castle refused to surrender, a great slaughter ensued. This continued until Henry called a halt to the senseless killing of the civilian population.

The artillery train of Henry V went on to be deployed at several sieges in the Normandy region. These included Rouen, a town which had defensive artillery of exceptional quality, and managed to hold out for five months, before the garrison was starved out. Another siege was conducted at Cherbourg in 1419, with the town holding out for some six months. The men serving the artillery in the field were invariably placed in the open and therefore vulnerable to fire from the defenders. To protect them wooden structures of boards were

Recreated fifteenth-century gunner with wooden handled tool swabbing out the barrel with a wet cloth after firing. This was carried out in order to extinguish any burning ember and prevent accidental explosions during reloading.

erected and moved aside when they were ready to fire their cannon. Another protective structure was a wooden palisade, which did not afford much protection but did obscure the gunners' movements from archers. These gunners fired their cannons at low angles in order to weaken the town's walls by undercutting them to the point where they were so damaged they collapsed under their own weight. This was a tactic which became widespread in use and was employed by artillerymen many times to

Artillery of Henry V at the siege of Rouen in 1419, during the Hundred Years War.

Wheeled wooden screens, behind which gunners would load and prepare their weapons whilst protected from archers and early hand-gunners.

Illustration showing the depiction of a French town c. *1500. The gunners are operating from behind wooden shields to protect them from hand-gunners and archers.*

Gunners using wooden screens to shield themselves from archers and hand-gunners.

breach walls using the easiest and simplest form of artillery fire with minimal risk to themselves.

Fourteen years after the Battle of Agincourt, a young French girl by the name of Jeanne d'Arc, which has been Anglicized over the years to read Joan of Arc, rose from obscurity to become a figurehead in the Hundred Years War. Born in 1412 to a peasant family, she later tended flocks of sheep until she began to experience religious visions. In 1429 she was given an audience with Charles, the Dauphin of France, and convinced him that she has been divinely inspired to rid France of the English. As a consequence of this meeting she was awarded the title *Chef de Guerre*. Her first action was to relieve Orléans, which was besieged by English forces. Both sides were using artillery, and the defenders of Orléans had seventy-one large cannons and many culverins. The Duke of Alencon stated that she was expert in 'the preparation of the artillery'. This is somewhat difficult to believe, given the fact that she had never received any formal military training. In his book *A History of Warfare*, Lord Montgomery of Alamein writes that he

has 'never been able to decide whether Joan had any God-given military ability herself or whether she was merely a tool in the hands of the French generals'. One is inclined to agree with the latter part of this statement, for men well versed in the use of artillery had considerable more experience than did Joan and they were many years her senior. Joan was captured by the English on 23 May 1430, whilst on her way to Compiegne. Tried and executed on 30 May 1431, her short-lived military career had spanned just fifteen months. Therefore, the Duke of Alencon's statement was probably just a reaffirmation of her God-fearing intentions, which did immense wonders for French morale and national pride.

The Battle of Formigny, 15 April 1450, was to be yet another engagement where French artillery provided victory. The French had learnt many lessons from earlier battles against the English, whom they were now defeating, and they had adopted different tactics. At Formigny, near to Bayeaux, the French commander, the constable de Richemont, deployed his troops beyond the range of the English archers, a force for which the French still held great respect. The French moved up two pieces of artillery called culverins, commanded by Giraud, the Master of Royal Ordnance, which were deployed to cover the flanks of the English Army. This was a force of 5,000 men under the command of Sir Thomas Kyriel and Sir Matthew Gough. A typical culverin could fire a 17lb (8kg) shot with some degree of accuracy out to 400yd (370m) range and the projectile would carry to a maximum range of 2,500yd (2,300m). The French cannon opened fire, inflicting severe casualties, and provoking an unplanned attack against the culverins, which the English succeeded in capturing. The French counter-attacked and Sir Thomas Kyriel's chevauchee was trapped and annihilated by superior forces. Despite the presence of French artillery at the battle it has been concluded that it was the arrival of some 2,000 reinforcements that decided the outcome and not artillery alone. The English left approximately 4,000 killed on the battlefield, including Sir Matthew Gough. It was now proven

that artillery, no matter how inaccurate, was a force to be reckoned with and over the following three years it was to grow in importance even further.

However, it was the Battle of Castillon, fought on 17 July 1453, just days before the French invested Bordeaux in siege, that would prove to be a significant turning point. Jean Bureau commanded a previously unheard of artillery force of 300 cannons, formed together into an area covering some 2,100ft (640m) wide by more than 600ft (183m) deep. The French force numbered 10,000 men, of which 700 were hand gunners to support their powerful artillery force. The English force of 6,000 was led by Sir John Talbot, Earl of Shrewsbury, who charged headlong and very impetuously at the French artillery park, no doubt with the intention of driving off the gunners. However, it is more than probable that the English force did not know the true strength of the French position. Opening fire the French inflicted heavy casualties among men and horses. During the charge a cannonball struck Sir John Talbot's horse, which fell to the ground in an awkward manner and pinned him under its full weight. In this state of utter helplessness, according to chroniclers, Talbot was killed by a blow from an axe wielded by a French man-at-arms. The English attackers were repulsed with great loss of life. The Battle of Castillon was the last engagement of the Hundred Years War, and in losing it not only did the English suffer another defeat, but they also lost the area of Gascony. Bordeaux surrendered on 19 October 1453 and the war was declared at an end, leaving only Calais remaining in English hands.

French victory is often credited to the development of gunpowder weapons. This is likely to be the case when considering the heavy siege artillery as commanded by the Bureau brothers, but at a tactical level, the results of deploying artillery were far from conclusive.

THE WARS OF THE ROSES

Left with only one possession in France, there was

no real reason for England to maintain a standing force for offensive purposes. Minor skirmishing and coastal raids between the countries continued, but in effect, England had become withdrawn and isolated from the mainstream of events unfolding on the European continent. This meant that the country was cut off from developments in the advancement of artillery and those weapons it did have in service would soon become outdated. This fact appears to have been overlooked and would soon be all but forgotten, as by 1455 the English had turned on themselves in a civil war for the throne of England. This was known as the Wars of the Roses, a political power struggle between the houses of Lancaster and York, who wore the red rose and white rose symbols respectively. Both claimed regency of England through descent from the sons of Edward III. In 1453 King Henry VI became ill and Richard, Duke of York, was created Protector of the realm. However Henry recovered, forcing Richard to take up arms in self-defence.

The war lasted for thirty years, with many minor engagements and sixteen major battles. The first clash of arms came at the Battle of St Albans on 22 May 1455 and the final came at the Battle of Bosworth on 22 August 1485. Both sides employed mercenary gunners recruited from various European states along with their artillery, which were deployed at a number of engagements with varying degrees of success.

For example, at the Battle of Tewkesbury, 4 May 1471, the Yorkist force commanded by Edward numbered over 4,000 troops. The terrain of the battlefield was difficult to traverse and Edward decided he would utilize his superiority in artillery and commence the battle with a prolonged bombardment 'with guns-shot as with shot of arrow'. The fighting was bloody, with victory going to the Yorkist army of Edward. The Lancastrian army had numbered 3,000 and after the fighting they left some 2,000 dead on the battlefield. It was becoming increasing clear that it was the army with the greatest artillery that would win the battle. The war continued for a further fourteen years before culminating in the Battle of Bosworth on 22

August 1485. The skills and knowledge which the mercenary gunners possessed virtually guaranteed their wellbeing, even if captured by the opposing side. The welfare of the families and labourers accompanying the gunners were also guaranteed, because it was realized that they too had the capability to operate the cannons.

By 1485, Henry Tudor, Duke of Richmond, had inherited the Lancastrian claim to the throne, and returning from exile landed at Milford Haven in Wales with a force of 3,000 French mercenaries, including gunners. Gathering supporters to his cause, and avoiding interception by Yorkist forces, he began to march on London. The Yorkist army, led by Richard III, numbered some 12,000 and moved to intercept the Lancastrian force, which by the time they met at Bosworth numbered at least 10,000. The battle began with Richard's artillery firing against the Lancastrian forces, but the artillery did not contribute much in the overall way the fighting developed. Even though both sides had gunpowder weapons they were also still using longbowmen and men-at-arms equipped with pikes. This reflected the old-fashioned ideas in fighting held in England and the country's reluctance to fully accept gunpowder weapons, especially artillery. As the two armies closed at Bosworth, Richard was killed as he attempted to force his way through to Henry, presumably for personal combat. The Lancastrian army mounted a flanking attack that caused the Yorkist army to flee, leaving behind some 900 dead.

However, the Lancastrian losses were of the order of only 100 men, which might imply that artillery was not a decisive factor in this conflict. The Lancastrian victory led to the conclusion of what was essentially a civil war and established Henry Tudor as King Henry VII of England. The Tudor dynasty was destined to last until 1603, during which time the country's fortunes were to ebb and flow. Only ten years after the Battle of Bosworth the king's list of artillery in the Tower of London is given by Sir Richard Guilford as including falcons, serpentines, curtow, demi-curtow and bombardelle, which fired balls ranging in size

Recreated fifteenth-century gunners showing the process of flushing out burning embers from the barrel after firing. This was necessary to prevent an explosion when loading the weapon for further firing.

from 1lb (0.5kg) to more than 260lb (120kg). But despite the success of Henry VII in war, it was his son, Henry VIII, who took the power of England's artillery train to new strengths.

FIELD ARTILLERY

This period in the history of artillery belongs to the French, for it was they who continued to lead the field and introduce newly-designed field artillery which would come to dominate the European battlefields in the final decade of the century. The new design for a light cannon with a barrel made from cast bronze and mounted on a two-wheeled carriage which could easily pulled by horses, began appearing around 1460. The cast bronze barrels were more expensive than traditional cast iron, but they were much safer to use and the design soon come to replace many of the older cannons. The first wooden gun carriages were fitted with large wheels, which initially were solid in design but later became the 'spoked' type, and demanded the skilled services of carpenters and labourers.

Early carriage designs had four wheels, but this was later reduced to two wheels, greatly improving manoeuvrability on the battlefield. These car-

Recreated fifteenth-century gunners loading a serpentine weapon in a representation of a battle from the time of the Wars of the Roses.

riages had to be light enough to be moved around by the men and yet strong enough to survive the stresses induced during firing. The carriage was built up in parts and comprised of 'cheek' or side bracket pieces which took the direct weight of the barrel when mounted. All parts of the carriage were interlocked and joined by means of interstices on their inner faces, which allowed them to be formed into the trail. Part of the carriage was called the bed, which formed part of the trail and allowed the secure fitting of the axletree, to which the wheels were fitted. The joints were strengthened by fitting metal straps, which were bolted into place. As gunpowder weapons developed into distinct roles on the battlefield, so too would these carriages evolve to take into account the requirements of a range of weapons including field, siege and garrison artillery.

With the mobility of its field artillery greatly improved, the French showed how it could be quickly deployed about the battlefield. In fact, it was becoming increasingly clear that it was the speed with which an army could deploy its artillery into action from the marching column that would

play a crucial role in the outcome of a battle. This was demonstrated by the French at the Battle of Fornovo in 1495, when they deployed a force of 1,000 artillerymen.

But it appears the French were not the only ones formulating the innovation of mounting cannons on wheeled carriages. In 1456, an Act of the Scottish Parliament passed a motion for barrels of artillery to be mounted on wheeled carriages for conveying light pieces of artillery, known as carts of war. Given the fact that Scotland and France had long enjoyed a close association, it is possible that there may have been an exchange of ideas which resulted in the development of the gun carriage.

The large pieces of artillery used in siege operations could be of extraordinary size and weight, which precluded them from free movement on the battlefield. Once sited in position they were forced to remain there for the duration of the engagement. This problem of size was compounded when such artillery had to be moved over great distances to accompany the army on campaign. The introduction of lighter pieces mounted on wheeled carriages from which they could also be fired, as in the

Recreated fifteenth-century gunner, showing how they operated the artillery in their charge without the encumbrance of armour, except for helmet. Dressed in this manner, they loaded and fired the guns and moved them from one location to another.

A very neat representation of fifteenth-century artillery massed against a castle's walls. Note the light armour worn by the gunners standing behind the artillery.

case of the French developments, went some way to remedying this problem. However, in the fifteenth century most roads were simply nothing more than well-worn routes along which passed all manner of traffic. In the dry months the surfaces of these roads were firm and could be traversed fairly easily. However, in wet conditions they were transformed into swamps, compounded by thousands of men and wagon-wheels as an army on the move traversed the route.

By now, artillery was an incontrovertible part of many armies and the men serving the cannons were gaining recognition as professionals in their own right. One uncertain aspect, however, remained and that was the drivers who handled the transport of the cannons, who were still civilians under contract to the army. This situation could and often did lead to all manner of complications. Should the campaign be considered too dangerous, the civilian drivers, who also owned the draught animals, would abandon the army, taking their assistants and the transport with them. This could happen at a crucial stage in the campaign and leave

the artillery stranded. However, if a military commander had hired gunners from those plying their trade as mercenaries, it was sometimes the case the contractor also owned the draught animals to haul the guns. This was a much better arrangement and ensured the service and loyalty of the gunners as long as they were paid. The contractual arrangement with civilians would remain in place for the time being and would not be ended until late in the sixteenth century, when drivers began to be recruited as part of the army and paid a soldier's wage.

The men operating the cannons were obliged to march alongside their weapons which meant that a slow walking pace, about 2mph, would the best speed to be hoped for from an artillery train. Horses were the obvious choice for use as animals to pull the guns, but whilst they had speed they lacked the stamina required to haul very heavy loads over poorly-maintained routes. The alternative was to use oxen, which were more hardy beasts of burden, but their speed was poor. A difficult choice between speed and endurance had to be made. However, in most cases the decision was likely to

Illustration showing a typical battle of the fifteenth century, in which artillery is used alongside other traditional weapons, including halbards and archers.

have been governed by the actual number of suitable animals available. In addition to the cannon, wagons were required for the transportation of ammunition and gunpowder and these also required draught animals.

Depending on the energies of the transport teams, artillery could filter on to the battlefield or arrive at the site of siege long after the main elements of the army had deployed. Estimates based on the sizes and weights of artillery during the fifteenth century have calculated that an artillery train containing 100 cannons, 60 mortars and 3,000 wagons would have required some 15,000 horses. Such a conglomeration would have been stretched out over 15 miles (24km) of road and would have taken many hours to pass one spot or even to arrive and assemble on the battlefield. This

Recreated gunners of the fifteenth century, showing how they must have loaded and worked the artillery of the period.

is not such a difficult situation to imagine, especially when one considers that some English cannons at this time were so large that they required an average of fifty horses to haul them. In such circumstances, even twelve such cannons would have required 600 horses alone, without considering those required to transport gunpowder and ancillary equipment.

ARTILLERY TRAINS

Artillery trains of exceptionally large size at this time are not difficult to conceive. For example, at the Battle of Morat on 22 June 1476, the Swiss are believed to have deployed some 10,000 culverins of various calibres, including some hand-held types. At this engagement Charles the Bold, leading a Burgundian army of 20,000 men, besieged Morat, near Bern and Fribourg, and constructed defensive positions with palisades and dug trenches. However, due to poor weather conditions the Burgundians had only managed to entrench about 4,000 men, with the remainder being encamped nearby. The Swiss army of 25,000, supported by 1,000 German and Austrian cavalry, attacked with great rapidity and inflicted losses of between 7,000 and 10,000 on the French. By contrast, only three months earlier, on 2 March 1476, at the Battle of Granson, the Swiss had attacked without artillery, even though the French positions were protected with artillery. The battle on that occasion had developed so quickly that the French were unable to deploy their artillery. The war between France and Switzerland began when the Swiss, fearing French ambitions on the Alsace border, allied itself with Austria and the Habsburgs to counter these advances, and the fighting dragged on for a further two years. The two sides clashed again on 5 January 1477 at the Battle of Nancy, where Charles the Bold was killed.

The number of gunpowder weapons deployed on the battlefield was on the increase and was beginning to show how a well-disciplined army so armed could inflict devastating losses on an army to which it might otherwise be numerically inferior. During their war against France, the Swiss, having apparently reconsidered their reluctance to accept gunpowder weapons, made great use of captured Burgundian artillery and deployed them against their former owners. One such type of artillery which the Swiss acquired in large numbers were wrought-iron field guns mounted on two-wheeled carriages. These were some of the older style French weapons, bound with iron hoops for strength, with a calibre of 75mm (3in). The overall length of these weapons was approximately 12ft (3.7m) and they were light enough to be dragged by two men using ropes attached to the trail of the carriage. The barrel was about 6ft (1.8m) in length and the elevation was adjusted by means of a bracket on the side of the carriage into which could be fitted pegs to support the frame on to which the barrel was mounted. The Burgundian artillery train was considered by many to be the finest in Europe, but against this the ferocious reputation of the Swiss in battle, particularly in defence of their homeland, made them a feared enemy. Such was this reputation and the known fact that they killed their enemy rather than take them prisoners, meant that such battles resulted in enemy forces frequently refusing battle. Here then, was a force which had originally scorned the use of artillery, but had finally realized its unstoppable force and taken such weaponry into service for its own ends.

Groups of gunners or individuals, along with their families, who owned their own artillery weapons were frequently hired as mercenary units, by the cities, states and monarchs who offered the best rates of pay and service conditions. The city of Nuremberg was armed with one particularly large piece of artillery which was named 'Chriemhilde', and probably dates from the early part of the fifteenth century. On its own, the barrel of this weapon weighed in excess of 600lb (270kg) and required a team of twelve horses to pull it. The frame onto which it was mounted for firing required a team of sixteen horses. The artillery train of Chriemhilde also included four wagons each car-

The siege of Ribodane, c. 1480. This shows attackers using artillery to cover their advance and also a wooden tower known as a 'befry' or 'belfry' to advance towards the walls of the castle.

rying eleven stone balls and a further five wagons were used to transport the cannon's ancillary equipment, such as tools and loading equipment, and gunpowder. It is known that this weapon, along with an experienced crew, was often loaned out to various cities and states, in return for a payment of money. Exactly when Chriemhilde was built is not entirely certain, but as early as 1414 it is recorded as having been hired out by Frederick of Nurem-

berg to the Teutonic Knights to breach the walls of the castles of the Brandenburg nobility. The problem with loaning out such artillery was the danger that the borrowers could turn it against the weapon's owners, but this was a risk which a number of city states were prepared to take.

During the closing years of the fifteenth century in Europe, the French introduced another innovation to artillery in the simple form of the trunnion. This part of the cannon is formed by horizontal axles protruding from either side of the barrel and resting in recesses on the carriage, thereby supporting the weight of the barrel and allowing the force of the recoil on firing to be passed into the carriage. The design of the trunnion, taken from the French word *trognon*, meaning stump, allowed for the mounting of cannon on wheeled carriages dedicated to a specific barrel. This invention gave improved aiming and accuracy in ranging, because for the first time the barrel could be elevated independently of the carriage. This was in sharp distinction to the earlier awkward methods of raising and lowering the muzzle or breech of the weapon. The idea soon spread and barrels of cannons were soon being cast with the trunnions as part of the design. The barrels of older cannons were up-graded by retro-fitting them with trunnion rings, a ring shrunk on to the barrel and fitted with trunnions to adapt them for use from a wheeled carriage.

Recreated fifteenth-century gunners at the point of actually firing their weapon. When fired, it would produce great clouds of smoke which would obscure the view and choke the gunners.

Recreated fifteenth-century gunners. They are representative of the period and show how families, including women, were used to serve the guns.

Above   *Detail of dolphins and trunnions on the barrel of a sixteenth-century Austrian bronze gun. These two features made handling and control of the barrel in elevation much easier.*

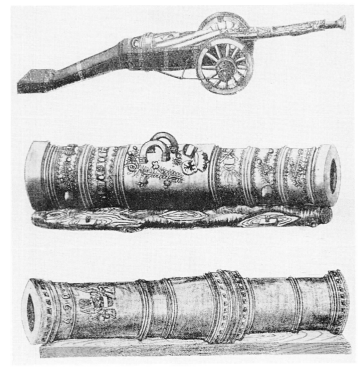

Artillery of Emperor Maximilian I of Austria in the sixteenth century. This image shows the falcon or basilisk at the top and examples of what appear to be bombards based on a design used by Turkish artillery of 1453, with the capstan bar spaces for unscrewing the gun at the bottom. Note also the dolphin lifting handles on the middle weapon.

Overall length of cast bronze Austrian barrel of the sixteenth century. The trunnions and dolphins are by this time an integral part of the barrel, and featured in designs used across Europe.

FRANCE VERSUS ITALY

In 1494, Charles VIII of France led an expedition into Italy on the premise of recapturing Constantinople or Jerusalem from the Moslems. His force of 25,000 included 8,000 Swiss mercenaries and his artillery train has been estimated to have contained between 266 and 300 weapons, of which seventy were of exceptional size. Such a force was capable of defeating all manner of targets, and naturally startled several European states into taking action against him. One of the first castles to fall to his artillery was the medieval Neapolitan castle of Monte San Giovanni, which had previously withstood a siege of traditional methods for a period of seven years. Within three hours of opening fire the castle had fallen to the forces of Charles VIII. The method used by the French gunners was to fire their artillery, using iron cannon balls, at the base of the walls of the castle and smash gaping holes in them. When the holes were large enough the walls became weakened to the point where they collapsed under their own weight. So effective at breeching walls was this technique that it continued to be used until well into the sixteenth century.

Within three months of starting his campaign most of Italy was in his grasp. Indeed, the

An English sixteen-century saker showing the barrel fitted with trunnions, but no dolphins in the casting. Sakers were used at sea on ships of the line and at sieges of walled cities.

Detail showing trunnions of a larger bronze cast barrel with lifting rings for handling when mounting on its carriage.

campaign has been described by the great Niccolo Machiavelli as being conducted 'chalk in hand'. This was because whatever Charles VIII marked on the map his gunners soon secured for him. In return for these successes, the French king was generous and paid his gunners at the daily rate of 5 to 6 livres. Such was the organization of the French army that it has come to be termed as the 'first modern army' due to the fact that all three service arms, infantry, cavalry and artillery, were co-operating together on the battlefield in co-ordinated tactics.

One of the last engagements during this excursion into Italy came when the French fought an Italian force of over 21,000 men, supported by some artillery, at Fornovo on 6 July 1495. The French artillery was highly efficient, having been modernized and the crews trained during years of continuous improvement and development. They were also highly experienced from earlier victories and were confident. The resulting battle was another French victory, with the artillery to the forefront of the action, with the Italians leaving over 3,500 dead on the battlefield. Some sources claim that it was the fact that French artillery fitted with trunnions helped to provide the victory. This is unlikely, since on its own the trunnion was but a single feature. However, when one takes into account the other advances made by the French to their artillery, such as bronze barrels and the improved manoeuvrability due to the two-wheeled carriage, its presence at the battle must have been a deciding factor. Certainly French artillery could be easily moved to cover different arcs of fire and the barrels elevated to engage targets at differing ranges, which was not available to the Italian artillery. For

Recreated fifteenth-century bombard resting on its wooden telaria platform. The wooden-handled tools are shown which are representative of the period and include rammers and swabs for washing out the barrel between firings to prevent premature explosion of the charge.

all of this, however, Commines has recorded that only twelve Italians were killed by artillery fire, which must be seen as an attempt to play down the importance of the French artillery.

STRENGTHENING DEFENCES

Castles and fortified towns had long been the ideal, if not natural target, against which artillery could be deployed. The French in their various campaigns had proven how vulnerable these defences could be against the concentrated power of artillery. This lesson had not been missed and the walls of such defences were in the process of either being built or remodelled with a more scientific approach in mind. They were now being built with a very thick construction to permit cannon to be fired from ramparts or specially constructed vaults within the walls. The most simple and common move was the creation of cannon-ports in the lower floors of towers, by converting existing arrow loops. Some castles were redesigned to allow for smaller pieces of artillery to be fitted to swivel mounts in the upper levels of the walls. These swivel-mounted cannons, sometimes called slings, were usually of the breech-loading type using the pre-loaded pots which were secured in place by a transverse wedge. They were fitted with a tiller-like projection at the breech-end to aid in aiming and could be over 4ft in length. They were used in the anti-personnel role against enemy troops, firing down stairs or through doorways. In fact, so useful were such weapons that they were also fitted to warships for use in repelling enemy sailors trying to board the ship. The design even found its way to the Far East, no doubt introduced by the seamen who sailed to these destinations for trade.

Swivel gun of sixteenth century. Breech loading in design, it was a handy weapon and easy to use. It could be fitted to ships for close quarter action and mounted at vulnerable points of defensive fortifications, such as doorways and stairs. The firing chambers could be stored preloaded with projectiles, including langridge as a type of early giant shotgun.

Detail of breech of swivel gun. Pre-loaded chambers could be quickly inserted and the weapon fired. It would have helped turn the tide of any attack launched within a confined space.

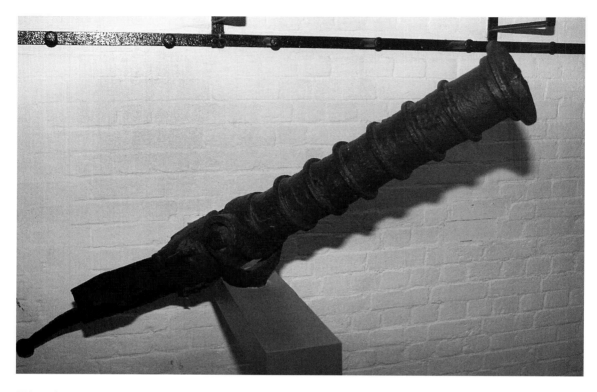

Fifteenth-century swivel gun of the breech-loading style. This type of weapon was mounted on ships for close actions and also to protect stairways in castles.

In an effort to reduce vulnerability to cannon fire, castle walls were made thicker at the base, and permanent outworks were constructed at a distance from the main walls. From such positions cannons and lighter firearms could be emplaced and used by defenders during a siege. These modifications were not universal and in the beginning were generally unusual outside France and Italy. In England, for example, with only internal national boundaries, to mark the borders of Scotland and Wales, it was perceived that there was no need to strengthen existing castles. However, internal fighting such as the Wars of the Roses and localized threats would lead to a gradual redesigning of such castles. Indeed, by the end of the century, artillery had all but rendered obsolete those traditionally-built medieval European fortifications.

The tall, straight walls were a target just waiting to be attacked by gunners, and the walls provided nowhere for large cannons suitable for counter-battery operations to be sited.

Forward-thinking architects, such as Giuliano da Sangallo, were already laying out plans for defensive measures. One of the first such specialized designs appears in the work completed at the Poggio Imperiale in Tuscany which incorporates a feature called the 'angle bastion'. Work on these defences started in the 1480s and features thick walls which have a squat shape and are broad triangular platforms, angled to present glancing surfaces to deflect the projectiles of attacking artillery. The design is such that when a city is ringed by such defences, it is afforded all-round defence, with each position capable of supporting one another. Such is the steep angle of the walls that the attacker is confronted with a formidable target which has little or no protective features at the base of its walls. The angle bastions also allowed defenders to site counter-battery artillery in prepared locations to fire back at the attacker. From now on, cities could fight back, and from their positions behind the walls the gunners could reload in relative safety.

THE HUSSITES

Other proponents of artillery to rise to pre-eminence were a group of people known as 'Hussites', who came from an unexpected quarter in the first part of the fifteenth century. The Hussites were from Bohemia and were followers of Jan Huss, who was burnt at the stake in 1415 at Constance, for his heretical Protestant beliefs. In 1419 the Bohemian followers of Huss rose in religious revolt against the Roman Catholic Emperor Sigismund, who was forced to form a large army to crush the movement and establish his authority. This was the start of what has become known as the Hussite Wars, essentially a religious war, lasting from 1419 until 1436. Although their natural leader had been killed four years earlier, rather than falling apart the Hussites rallied to the command of Jan Ziska (sometimes called John Ziska), an experienced and capable military leader, and under his leadership continued to resist Sigismund. One of their first military engagements came on 30 July, when the Hussites arrived to give assistance to the city of Prague which was being besieged by Sigismund. On Vitkov Hill, Ziska established a defensive position which he called a wagenburg. Sigismund attacked this formation and was bitterly repulsed by the well-sited Hussites, and had to withdraw from Bohemia. On entering the city they discovered four particular cannons in the castle, the design of which so greatly impressed Ziska that he ordered them to be copied and distributed throughout his forces. It may well have been these weapons on which the Hussites based the pieces of artillery known as 'snakes' which equipped the wagenburg.

Sigismund was the stepbrother of Wenceslas IV of Bohemia, and was never a popular figure. In fact it was to be seventeen years before he was recognized by the Bohemians. Following his defeat, Sigismund's cause against the Hussites was given support in March 1420, when Pope Martin V declared a Bohemian Crusade against the Hussites. With this support he returned in 1421, only to be defeated by Ziska's wagenburgs defences at the battles of Lutitz and Kuttenberg, fought on 6 and 9 of January respectively. Sigismund fielded mainly cavalry units and the Hussites were to show how artillery could be used as another means to defeat this elite force.

The wagenburg tactics employed by the Hussites involved the use of mobile wagon forts, formed into travelling units, from which they could defend themselves. It was a formidable formation and would go on to influence other military units. The development of the wagenburg is credited to Jan Ziska, and it showed how field artillery could be used by a mobile group to form part of the emerging all arms force. The tactic was really quite simple, with the Hussites protecting themselves within the wagenburgs when travelling across open expanses of countryside. The wagenburgs were formed from the group's horse-drawn wagons which were protected with armour and equipped with openings cut in their sides through which men could fire their weapons. The success of the wagenburg lay in the group's ability to use the wagons as armoured positions by gathering them together in either a circle or square, to form a base from which they could fight. For added strength the wagons could be joined together by chains to prevent the enemy from turning one over or rolling it away. A further refinement was to dig a defensive ditch around the formation, but this was only undertaken if time permitted. The Hussites were a self-contained group, to the point of even possibly having members who were skilled gunsmiths. A sketch dated around 1430 purports to show a wagenburg with a mobile ore-crushing device for making iron, which would have permitted them to make and repair their own cannon. When Ziska died in 1424 his legacy was such that the Hussite successes continued, and survived through the campaigns of 1426–1427, and they even pushed into Germany where they fought pitched battles at Aussig and Tachau.

The wagenburg formation was further refined by placing armed men either in the wagons or the gaps in between them, in order to provide all-round defence. Light cannons, known as 'snakes' and possibly of the type copied from the castle in Prague, were also sited in these intervals between the wagons, to increase their firepower. The combined firepower from these strategically placed weapons permitted the Hussites to concentrate

Illustration showing the method used by the Hussites to form up their wagenburg in the defensive tactic. It shows light guns placed among the wagons which would have wreaked havoc against attacking cavalry and infantry.

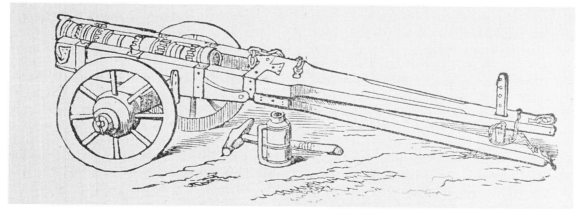

Fifteenth-century artillery with the barrel attached to a wheeled carriage and fitted with early means of elevation. This may have been of the type used by the Hussites in their wagenburgs.

their fire quickly and easily to cover any quarter from wherever they were threatened. Whenever possible the Hussites built up mounds of earth within the wagenburg on which they placed their artillery mounted on wheeled carriages, although this could only be done if they were warned in advance of an actual attack. Thus their artillery protected the wagenburg and the infantry protected the cannons. Such a concentration of forces consistently defeated the attacks mounted against them by German, Hungarian and Polish cavalrymen and infantrymen. Once the impetus of any such attack had been broken, Hussite cavalry forces would launch a counterattack which was often pressed home with considerable zeal. On 6 January 1422, for example, when Sigismund attacked the Hussites at Nebovid, as they were isolated outside Kutna Hora, he discovered the intensity of their counterattack. Ziska's troops mounted a night attack of such force that they not only succeeded in penetrating Sigismund's command but also broke his will to fight such a well-defended enclave.

Just as religious differences had led to the creation of the Hussites forces, so it led to their final defeat. At the Battle of Lipani on 16 June 1434, the Taborite faction of the Hussites were defeated by the combined forces of the nobles and the Utraquists, which in turn led to the re-establishment of the monarchy. But that was not the end of the wagenburg as a tactical manoeuvre, as it was taken up by the Hungarians who modified it for their own purposes in their campaigns against the Ottoman Turks. Ziska's tactical thinking did not lead directly to the introduction of light field artillery, but he had shown how light cannons could be used during offensive or defensive operations and support combined arms on the battlefield. The Hussites may not have developed new types of weaponry, but as Sir John Fortescue wrote of Ziska's tactics:

> Throwing all military pedantry to the winds, Ziska fought as his own genius dictated. He was the first to make artillery a manoeuvrable arm, the first to

execute complicated evolutions in the face of the enemy and the first to handle cavalry, infantry and artillery in efficient tactical combination.

In short, then, Ziska's wagenburg tactic was forward thinking, and future military leaders would study his tactics for years to follow.

DEVELOPMENTS OUTSIDE EUROPE

Despite the great amount of activity in Europe during the fifteenth century, one must not overlook the

A wooden wagon, probably pushed by infantry, used to position the device in a location where the troops could bring the fire of their artillery and handguns to bear with better effect. Very simple, it is of a type used by archers for hundreds of years.

advances being made by countries in the Far East, such as China. Either by design or accident some of the developments paralleled some European achievements and at times even overtook them in terms of advancement. During the sixth year of the T'ien Sun reign, 1462, Chinese chroniclers record how some 1,200 gun carriages were built. Only three years later, in 1465 during the first year of the Ch'eng-Hua reign, 500 carriages for cannons were built and 300 'great general guns' were manufactured. Such figures, along with others, lead to the conclusion that Chinese manufacture of artillery may have been far more advanced than in Europe. In fact, such was the resource of the country that on its own China was capable of producing a far greater output than all European countries combined, and on a scale of almost mass-production.

One particular weapon in use in China was a design known as a 'great general gun'. According to records the barrel weighed almost 180lb (82kg), and was fitted to a bronze carriage weighing more than 1,300lb (590kg). This may seem rather disproportionate and one has to take into account possible inconsistencies in translation over the years. Accounts tell us that it had a range of 800 paces and fired a lead shell, known as a 'Grandfather shell', which weighed almost 8lb (3.6kg). It could also fire a shell of some 4lb, known as a 'son shell', and a third shell of only 2lb was known as a 'grandson shell'. The Grandfather shell contained some 200 small projectiles, weighing between 2 and 3oz (57–85g), and these were called 'grandchildren bullets'. This gave rise to the Chinese saying that the 'grandfather' leads the way and the 'grandchildren' follow. This projectile is of the type that would become known as either case or canister shot. It is not surprising that the Chinese should have perfected this type of projectile, because as early as 1410 such case or canister shot is known to have been used in Europe.

Other Chinese projectiles were supplemented with iron and porcelain fragments, similar to langridge which had been used in Europe during the fourteenth century. However, because the Chinese were known to have previously boiled these

fragments in cantharides beetle poison, it can also be viewed as an early form of chemical warfare weapon. Some projectiles fired from Chinese weapons containing such fragments weighed 26lb (12kg), which is relatively light, but a single shot is recorded as having 'the power of a thunderbolt, causing several hundred casualties among men and horses'. This high casualty rate is not surprising because even a scratch inflicted by the poisonous fragments would have been fatal.

The Chinese are known to have also developed a double-barrelled cannon known as 'Mr Facing-Both-Ways' which comprised of two cannons joined together at the breech-ends. When one barrel had been fired it was simply rotated to permit the crew to fire the second barrel. A Chinese account of the weapon in actual use states:

> Immediately after firing the first gun the second is rotated into position and fired, each one being muzzle loaded with a stone projectile. If the gun is aimed at the hull of an enemy ship below the waterline, the cannon-balls shoot along the surface and smash the side into splinters. It is a very handy weapon.

Of all the Far Eastern countries China was undoubtedly the most powerful in terms of artillery. By the fifteenth century it is recorded that the artillery force of a single battalion in the Chinese army included some 40 batteries of cannons, 3,600 'thunder-bolt shells', 160 'wine-cup muzzle-loading general cannons', 200 large and 328 small 'continuous bullet cannons', 624 hand guns, 300 small grenades and almost 9,000lb of gunpowder and over 1,050,000 bullets. This impressive inventory of weaponry has lead Dr Joseph Needham to remark that 'this was quite some firepower, and the total weight of the weaponry was reckoned to be 29.4 tons'. It was the vastness of China which required the rapid development of a powerful range of gunpowder artillery, in order to maintain the country's security. In the early years of gunpowder development, its isolation meant that such technology remained secret for some time. But over a period of time and the expansion of trade routes the news of such advances, particularly weaponry, was soon transferred from one civilization or country to another. And so it must be concluded that western European countries were able to develop a wide diversity of gunpowder weapons for themselves, that in many ways paralleled China's technology.

OVERSEAS EXPLORATION

The fifteenth century was also the century of exploration with many new territories being discovered. Between 1492 and 1502 Christopher Columbus sailed four voyages that explored much of the Caribbean Sea. He claimed his discoveries for Spain, which included San Salvador, Cuba and Central and South America, all very rich in gold, spices and other riches. In 1498 Vasco da Gama of Portugal reached India, where they had an understanding of gunpowder artillery, and Ferdinand Magellan circumnavigated the world. With them they took gunpowder weapons for self-protection

including some light cannons. Some of these may have been weapons of a type called sakers which could fire a 5lb (2.3kg) shot with reasonable accuracy out to 350yd (320m). Sakers had a maximum range of 1,700yd (1,600m), which was far greater than any weapon likely to be encountered on such voyages of exploration where primitive tribes were armed with bows and arrows. Such an increase in naval activity meant that there was often an overspill from the wars involving leading European countries, and led to a conflict of interests in overseas territories.

THE CHANNEL ISLANDS

It was not just the very rich lands with their gold reserves which had to be defended by the ruling nation. Even very small islands found themselves having to be defended by artillery. For example, the Channel Islands, English possessions lying just off the coast of France, were considered to be extremely vulnerable to attack by France and were therefore armed in accordance to meet such a

Mont Orgueil castle on Jersey in the Channel Islands. One of the early medieval castles to be modified to take gunpowder artillery in specially built defensive positions called batteries.

threat. Between 1435 and 1436 Gorey Castle at Mont Orgueil on the island of Jersey was repaired and strengthened to accept cannons. Despite this, however, the French did seize the island and held it from 1461 until 1468, during which time Pierre de Breze, Count of Maulevrier, Grand Seneschal of Normandy, ordered that Guy de Briouse, acting as Governor of Gorey Castle, prepare a list of the castle's ordnances. The inventory, compiled in 1462, states that he is to inspect 'often all the armaments of the place, cannons, culverins, crossbows, cannon balls and powder'. This shows that England was attempting to protect its overseas possessions, even those closest to home ports. The island of Jersey was secured once more for England in 1468 by Vice Admiral Richard Harliston and Philip de Carteret. To mark the occasion The Harliston Tower, essentially an artillery platform, was specially built to protect the castle at Gorey and help defend the anchorage below Mont Orgueil. As the fifteenth century closed, such defences were soon to be found around the globe as each maritime nation established artillery forces to secure and consolidate its overseas interests. These would be tested and further strengthened during the sixteenth century as nations once more came into conflict.

4   Into a New Period: 1500 to 1600

Mainland Europe at the start of the sixteenth century was an extremely unsettled place with border wars and internal quarrels, some of which were a continuation of disputes that had started in the fifteenth century. In effect, therefore, the new century started the same way as the previous century had ended. One of the first battles to be fought was between Spain and France at Cerignola over the question of Italian conquest. France and Spain had clashed several times during the closing years of the previous century, which had often resulted in Spanish victories. Spain had adopted handguns before many other European states and modified their strategy to give them a tactical advantage.

SPAIN VERSUS FRANCE

In 1503, Louis XII of France was pursuing Italian conquest as begun by Charles VIII nine years earlier. The Spanish sent a force of 6,000 men into France commanded by Hernandez Gonzalo de Cordoba, who had bitter experience of fighting the French, having been defeated by them several years earlier. He knew that to gain a conclusive victory his army must have more gunpowder weapons and dig protective earthworks. On 21 April 1503, the two sides met at the Battle of Cerignola. The Spanish force had marched from Barletta and taken up position in trenches on a hillside behind a protective palisade of sharpened wooden stakes. The Spanish artillery was rendered useless when its entire stock of gunpowder exploded. Undeterred, the Spanish stood firm in their prepared positions. Under the support of their artillery the

French, led by the Duke de Nemours, advanced their cavalry and mercenary Swiss pikemen in a frontal attack. Well-sited Spanish handgunners took a steady toll of the French, who were thrown back in confusion. Gonzalo ordered his cavalry to attack, and completed the rout. The Battle of Cerignola is seen as being the first military engagement to be won entirely by the use of gunpowder weapons and led to Cordoba being termed the 'Father of Trench Warfare'. However, the lesson was not lost on the French, who copied the Spanish methods of fighting and tried to create countermeasures against these methods. Other nations learning of this engagement also modified their battlefield tactics to take into account the new tactics of warfare with gunpowder weapons. European armies from this time onwards took steps towards creating professional forces and incorporating the developing advances being made in the field of artillery and other gunpowder weapons. This included infantry weapons, of the type used by Spain, and termed harquebuses or arquebuses, possibly after a corruption of the old German term *hake* meaning hook, which were fast replacing the longbow and other weapons used by traditional foot soldiers.

DEVELOPMENTS IN ENGLAND UNDER HENRY VIII

In England, Henry VII had emerged victorious from the Wars of the Roses and successfully reigned for twenty-four years. But on his death in 1509, and after years of virtually self-imposed

Illustration showing how artillery is being used to cover the advance of infantry as it approaches the town under attack. This is dated c. *1500, and shows how tactics were continually evolving.*

isolation, he bequeathed to his son an army that was poorly equipped to fight a war and had been allowed to fall into stagnation. The long years of seclusion had led to England falling behind in mainstream European military doctrines. However, for the energetic Henry VIII, at a youthful age of only eighteen years, this was not acceptable. Traditionally it was the task of the Master Gunner of England to organize the artillery train for deployment on a campaign along with the master gunners, their 'mates' and 'mattrosses'. Henry discovered that although the weapons existed and were kept in storage at the Tower of London, the actual artillery train was not in any state to be mobilized had a campaign been instigated.

Henry also discovered that he had no Master Gunner and he was shocked to learn that whilst England had many foundries that could cast bells, only one man, Humphrey Walker, had the experience and capability to cast barrels for artillery. Henry elected Walker to the post of Master Gunner at the Tower of London, with twelve other master gunners under his command, with the aim of instructing others in the art of gun founding and to train gunners. To redress the shortfall in his arsenal, Henry placed orders to purchase cannons from Hans Poppenruyter, the Master Founder of Malines. Henry may have been impetuous but he realized that in order to pursue any military ambitions he had to make preparations. In 1512, he acquired forty-eight pieces of artillery, in readiness for his first Continental military expedition. These came from the workshops of Hans Poppenruyter, and are known to have included sixteen guns weighing between 3,000lb (1,360kg) and 4,000lb (1,810kg) and twelve further in a range known as the 'Twelve Apostles'. The Netherlands also sold him draught horses, Flemish mares, at the rate of fourteen animals for each gun. The Exchequer Accounts records these were to allow for one animal per 250lb of gun, minus carriage.

With his artillery force reinforced, Henry felt confident enough to begin reclaiming those lost English possessions in France and re-establish English power on the Continent. He began his campaign in earnest when he landed his force of 28,000 men at Calais in June 1513. This town was still an English possession and although harassed by 15,000 French, they refused to give battle. The first engagement came several weeks later when the two sides met at the Battle of Guinegate, on 16 August 1513, but the artillery action was confined to the English army. It had been the intention of the French to send a relief force to the aid of Therouanne, but the English, with support from the

Imperialist forces of Emperor Maximilian I, fired on the column with artillery and scattered them. The French town of Therouanne had been invested by the besieging forces of Henry VIII and Emperor Maximilian in August 1513, which was to fall through the effects of their artillery. An English soldier recalled in a letter how:

> The walls of Turwyne [Therouanne] are sore beaten with gunnes and many houses broken and destroyed. Our gunnes lie within a birdbolt shote to the wallis and our miners are also near them.

The town was finally taken on 22 August and had proved Henry's faith in the power of his artillery force. Following this success, Henry moved his artillery train to Tournai which fell on 23 September, following a bombardment lasting eight days.

CONFLICTS IN SCOTLAND

At the time of Henry's involvement with France,

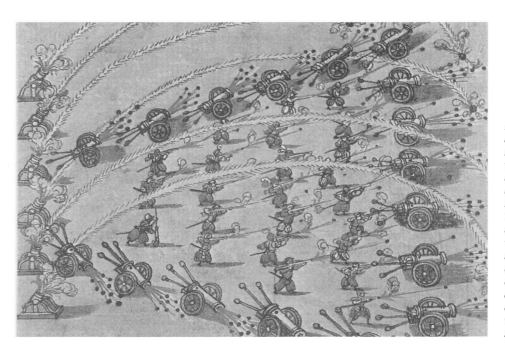

Field tactics of artillery and mortars working in co-operation with one another in bombardment. This action, if ever performed, would have smothered the enemy in the open or levelled any city or castle walls within a short space of time.

the Earl of Surrey was campaigning in Scotland, where he finally brought the forces of James IV to engagement at the decisive Battle of Flodden on the 9 September 1513. The battle opened with an artillery duel, and the English boldly, if somewhat rather rashly, attacked the Scottish forces strongly sited on Flodden Hill. Their tactics carried the day and James IV of Scotland and many of his principal nobles were killed. The Master Gunner in the Scottish army was Robert Borthwick, who was appointed to the position in 1511, and who had some seventeen pieces of artillery under his command at Flodden. Two of these were particularly large and had been transported from Threave Castle. They were probably of the old-fashioned bombard type, fired from static positions. James had taken a keen interest in artillery and prided himself on his force. At Flodden he had been well-prepared and his train had included thirteen carts, each carrying four barrels of gunpowder. Ammunition had been transported by twenty-eight pack horses carrying the projectiles in panniers. But for all this, the Scottish forces were still unable to gain a victory.

THE ARTILLERY TRAIN OF HENRY VIII

With his northern borders now secure, Henry was free to pursue his campaign in Europe and enter to into an alliance with Germany, Spain, Italy and the Pope with the aim of driving France out of Italy. The artillery train which Henry VIII had at his disposal was by no means the largest in Europe, but it was certainly one of the most impressive. By now the collective term for the preparation of artillery in readiness for a campaign was referred to as the 'Trayne', with individual weapons being called 'pieces of Ordnance', from where the descriptive term for a single weapon of artillery as a piece is derived. This later term is believed to have come about when Henry ordered an enquiry into the correct weights of his cannon. Weapons cast in a recognized manner were termed 'ordinance guns' and

afterwards became known as 'ordnance' with the letter 'i' dropped from the term.

In September 1523, Geoffrey Hughes drew up an inventory of Henry's artillery in storage at the Tower of London. This included seventy-four cannon, including seven large bombards, which fired cannon balls weighing some 250lb (110kg) using a charge of almost 80lb (36kg). We are told that each of these was hauled by twenty-four horses. If one remembers that one horse was allowed for pulling 250lb of each gun, then these large pieces in Henry's arsenal must have been in the order of 6,000lb (2,700kg). The same list mentions a number of small pieces known as falconets. The gunners serving these weapons were paid accordingly: 2 shillings per day for the bombards, and 8 pence per day for the falconets.

In 1547, another inventory was made of the military stores kept within the Tower of London and is listed by the chronicler Hall as being '5 great curtalls, 2 great culverynges, 4 sakers and 5 serpentynes, as fayre ordance as hathe bene, beside other smal peces'. This list included some cannons taken from the Scots at the Battle of Flodden in 1513.

The iron guns mentioned made up but a small part of the total of artillery pieces available to Henry's forces, many of which had been cast on the Continent. In 1559 we learn that the garrison at Mont Orgueil Castle on Jersey comprised of thirty-eight soldiers, including twelve gunners, each of whom was paid at the rate of 2 pence per day, and the gunners $2^{1}/_{2}$ pence per day. Henry was known to be 'indifferent' to handguns, but on the matter of cannons he took a personal interest and set out to establish a powerful force by acquiring 'cannon enough to conquer Hell'. Indeed, he showed his faith in artillery by creating an officer of state, the Master of the Ordnance, with his own department to attend to the provision and storage of artillery and ammunition for land forces and the navy. In 1537, he established the Guild of St George to be 'overseers of the science of artillerie', and it was to be that artillery which made the greatest contribution towards the defence of England.

Artillery of the fifteenth century being pushed into position to commence a siege. Note how gunners are dressed very lightly for their role.

Artillery of the fifteenth century deployed against a castle. Note the barrels of gunpowder and projectiles, which still appear to be stone balls. The gunners are dressed very lightly and they are covered by archers using longbows, and early hand-gunners.

EMPEROR MAXIMILIAN I OF GERMANY

It could be argued that Henry's direct counterpart in Europe was the Emperor Maximilian I of Germany, whose main cannon foundry was located at Innsbruck. The Emperor took a keen interest in his artillery during his reign and is known to have visited foundries to oversee his weapons being cast. Like Henry VIII, he also purchased bronze cannons, cast by Hans Poppenruyter and Remy de Hallut, from the southern provinces of the Netherlands, where Germany exercised power. Maximilian's arsenal was prepared over a four-year period from 1504 to 1508. Between 1515 and 1519 it was catalogued in detail by Wolfgang Reisacher at Innsbruck. The German court painter and architect, Jorg Kolderer, illustrated Maximilian's arsenals from 1507 until 1512. His scenes depict the Imperial artillery on the march with bronze cannons being drawn by teams of horses and forming up on the field. He shows bombards, which in Germany were called *hauptstucke*, and even a small falconet on a carriage light enough to be pulled by a single horse. Kolderer's illustrations also show what appears to be a four-wheeled wagon which served as a mobile stamping mill for 'corning' or milling gunpowder whilst on campaign.

An account of Maximilian's artillery train on campaign is detailed in the work *History of Bayard* by the 'Loyal Serviteur', Pierre du Terrail, Chevalier de Bayard, who writes:

> He had one hundred and five pieces of artillery on trucks, the smallest of which was termed a falcon, and six large bom-ketches, which could not be fired from off the gun-carriages, but were drawn on powerful wagons and accompanied by cranes, and when they wished to fire them they were placed on the ground, and with the crane was raised slightly the mouth of the piece, under which was placed a large piece of wood, and behind them placed a strong buttress to prevent recoil. These pieces fired off bullets of stone, of weight hardly to be lifted, and could only be fired

at most four times each day ... The Cardinal de Ferarra came in place of the Duke, his brother, to the Emperor's assistance, bringing with him twelve pieces of artillery, five hundred horses, and three thousand foot-men.

FRANCE

Campaigns of Gaston of Foix

France was still in deep military conflict with Italy, an action which had started in 1494 and was to become the major war in Europe. France found itself being attacked on the northern coast by England, and its western borders by Spain, so that it was fighting a war on three fronts. France had mixed fortunes in battle and all gunners were to learn much from the war which dragged on until 1559. In fact, the experience gained by gunners learned in these battles would be put to good use when they came to hire themselves out as mercenaries. The French had fought the Spanish at the Battle of Cerignola in 1503, and learned much. The next major engagement in the dispute over Italy came at the Battle of Ravenna on 11 April 1512, which is often described as the first confrontation between two truly modern field armies.

The fighting was now in its eighteenth year and this particular phase has come to known as the Campaigns of Gaston of Foix. The Count Gaston of Foix, the Duke of Nemours, at the age of only twenty-one was the French commander, and led his forces with a tireless energy. The first part of his campaign had started well when he fought off an Allied army and captured Bologna on 13 May 1511. Moving northwards towards Brescia, he defeated a force of Venetians and captured the city. By early 1512, with most of northern Italy under his command, Gaston turned south to invest Ravenna, which he reached in March the same year. He had under his command a force of 32,000 men, including some 8,500 mercenaries, supported with fifty-four cannons.

He found his way barred by a Spanish force of 18,000 men with thirty cannons, commanded by

Pedro Navarro, a military engineer by training. The Spanish were deployed with their rear protected by the River Ronco and their flanks well entrenched. The two sides engaged in an artillery duel, during which the Spanish cavalry suffered heavy casualties, but the infantry in their trenches were left almost untouched. Using his superior artillery to provide fire support, Gaston was able to transfer two cannons over the River Ronco in a flanking move. From here his gunners were able to fire into the rear of the Spanish positions. The French mounted a frontal assault, which, combined with their fierce artillery fire, unnerved the Spanish who broke ranks and fled their trenches. In the open they were easy targets for the French artillery which took toll of almost half their total force. The French had lost just 4,500 men, but their imaginative leader Gaston of Foix was killed.

The Fighting Continues

The Battle of Marignano in September 1515, was to prove a lesson from which every military thinker learned something. It showed how an impetuous force lacking artillery support, especially when facing a numerically superior enemy, will always be defeated. On 13 September a Swiss mercenary force of more than 22,000 attacked with such suddenness that the French were unable to bring their artillery into action. The French force of 32,500, led by Francis I, mounted a counter-attack which lasted five hours. On the morning of 14 September, the Swiss had reorganized and they resumed the battle with typical ferocity. The French had by now organized their artillery of 140 cannons which unleashed a concentrated fire into the Swiss ranks and inflicted heavy losses. The French had gained a victory but lost some 6,000 men. The Swiss, lacking artillery, had lost 12,500 men, with the result that they never fought outside of their national borders again as a fully organized army. The anti-French alliance collapsed, Francis I occupied Milan and France was in control of Lombardy.

If the Battle of Marignano had taught many lessons, then the Battle of La Bicocca on 27 April 1522 emphasized the fact that military leaders would need to greatly improve their tactics regarding artillery and harquebuses. The Battle of La Bicocca was the first major engagement between Charles V, the new Emperor of Germany and also King of Spain, and François I, King of France. Charles V claimed Milan and Burgundy while François claimed Navarre and Naples. The dispute was over the territorial question of Italy.

Sixteenth-century Italian artillery train on the march. Note draught animals hauling the artillery and carrying ammunition and powder casks.

The fighting would continue until 1559 with many engagements, but it was La Bicocca which stands out from the rest. The French force of some 25,000 with 10,000 allied Venetians and 8,000 Swiss mercenaries, commanded by Marshal Odet de Lautrec, was advancing on Milan in April 1522, when an Italian force of some 20,000, commanded by General Prosper Colona, deployed at Bicocca. The Italians with their Spanish arquebusiers established themselves in strong well-entrenched defensive positions. On the 27 April, the Swiss mercenary force, after some indecision and impatience in waiting for the supporting French artillery to be sited, attacked the Italian positions, where they suffered 3,000 casualties in less than half an hour. Lautrec was forced to withdraw eastwards into allied Venetian territory to recover.

This time, however, gunpowder weapons had dealt the Swiss such a severe blow that they could no longer afford to ignore advances in tactics and weapons. In future their mercenary units would never again use the old-fashioned tactic of attacking by frontal assault any position believed to be defended with artillery. Mercenaries hired their services out to the highest bidder, who recognized the formidability of such a cohesive and well-trained fighting force. The Swiss had long been considered the best infantry mercenaries because of their ruthlessness in battle, but they were inclined to act without thinking, much to their cost in lives. Another emergent mercenary force at the time was the German *Landsknechte*, who operated by a strict code of conduct, and their stability and experience was also greatly desired. Under their own rules, the *Landsknechte* could plunder and take prizes of war and loot, but they could not take gunpowder or artillery. These items of ordnance had to be handed over to the field captain.

Between January and February 1525, under the command of Francis I, a French force of 28,000, including 4,000 Swiss mercenaries, and supported with fifty-three cannons, besieged the city of Pavia in yet another engagement over Italy. The defenders of the city's garrison numbered some 6,000. A relieving Imperialist German force of 23,000, with seventeen cannons, under the command of Marquis of Pescara attempted to fight its way through to the city in January but found its way barred by French entrenchments and a river which could not be crossed. Unable to move forward, the Imperialist forces dug trenches and engaged in an artillery bombardment against the French, which achieved little or nothing.

In an attempt to break the deadlock, during the night of 24–25 February Pescara moved his Imperialist forces northwards using the combination of a storm and artillery bombardment to cover his movements. Pescara's troops managed to cross the river and attacked the left flank of the French positions. The French were surprised by the attack, but quickly mounted a spirited counter-attack. At first they gained ground but Spanish arquebusiers began to open accurate fire, which took a heavy toll. The garrison of Pavia then sallied out to launch an attack on the French troops in the trenches and managed to destroy them. The French artillery could not support the attacks because of the speed at which the battle had developed. In less than two hours the siege had been lifted and the French had lost 13,000 men killed or wounded, and all fifty-three pieces of artillery had been captured. The Imperialist forces had lost only 500 killed or wounded.

THE TURKISH FORCES

At around this time, on the other side of Europe, the Turks under the reign of Suleiman the Magnificent, the great-grandson of Mehomet II, began a campaign against the Christians on the Mediterranean island of Rhodes, which was fortified and garrisoned by Knights Hospitallers of St John. On 25 June 1522 the Turks carried out an amphibious landing of 100,000 men supported by siege engineers and artillery. By July the Turkish forces were in full siege positions with their artillery in place. They made repeated assaults, and in one month alone the Turkish artillery fired more than 3,000 cannon balls into the fortress. By December the

Turks had penetrated into the city's outer defences but they were repulsed with heavy losses. Suleiman made an offer of peace to the defenders in which he guaranteed their safety. He wanted to end the siege which was breaking down into a war of attrition, in which neither side would win. His proposals were accepted and the garrison evacuated to Malta. Out of an original force of 700 knights and 6,000 other troops, only 180 knights and 1,500 other troops, many of whom were wounded, were able to make their departure. The operation had cost Suleiman between 50,000 and 100,000 men from a force which had been reinforced to number some 200,000.

Over the next three years Turkey conducted an ongoing series of border wars against Hungary. In 1524 Suleiman entered into a pact with Poland which left the way open for him to directly attack Hungary with his full force, which he did in April 1526. On 29 August the two armies met at a site called Mohacs, close to the Danube River. The Turkish army numbered about 300,000 men with an artillery train containing 300 cannons. The Hungarian army had a mere 25,000 men with about 20 pieces of artillery. Outnumbered as they were 12:1 in men and 15:1 in artillery, it was a foregone conclusion that the Hungarian army would lose the battle. Although they had inflicted losses to the invading Turkish army, the Hungarians left 15,000 dead on the battlefield. The Turks were not as magnanimous at Mohacs as they had been at Rhodes and all Hungarian prisoners were decapitated. With their leaders dead, the Hungarian resistance crumbled and Suleiman's campaign was able to continue, and by 1529 he had entered Austria. He used the power of his siege artillery to reduce any town or city which resisted him.

Finally they arrived at Vienna, where the garrison was commanded by Marshal William von Roggendorf. From 27 September until 15 October the Turkish army invested Vienna but were unable to make any advances due to the garrison conducting an imaginative and spirited defence. Recognizing that the area where the Turkish forces formed up was a weak spot, von Roggendorf ordered that

the defenders direct their artillery in counter-bombardment against the Turkish artillery. This tactic was so successful that it completely disrupted the Turkish plans and they eventually withdrew having met a total impasse.

By 1533 Suleiman's attentions had turned eastwards towards Persia and, for the time being at least, an uneasy peace existed between Turkey and Hungary. Eleven years later, in 1544, Suleiman was forced to return to Hungary to fight King Ferdinand who had raised an army against him. The Turkish army was huge and the artillery train included 60 siege cannons, 80 field pieces with 200,000 cannon balls and 500 tons of gunpowder, moved by more than 1,000 horses. Again, Suleiman's forces were victorious and in his defeat King Ferdinand was forced to pay tribute for the small strip of northern and western Hungary which he was allowed to retain.

RESEARCH INTO SCIENTIFIC IMPROVEMENTS

Artillerymen in the sixteenth century were still facing the age-old problem of how best to combine mobility with long-range firepower. The French had made great strides to improve the mobility of artillery, and their gunners had reached a level of proficiency that was previously unknown, but little had been achieved to increase the overall effective range of the cannons. After a series of experiments it became clear to a number of diverse practitioners in the science of artillery that overall improvements in range, accuracy and firepower resulted from those weapons fitted with a barrel length of twenty calibres or more. That is to say, that if the diameter of the barrel was 4in, then the barrel length had to be twenty times that, which gave an overall length of 80in. The walls of these new types of barrels had to be thick enough to withstand the pressures built up by discharge of a large powder charge.

However, these experiments were not universally accepted and in 1521, Charles V of Brussels

The Turkish Artillery Train

During the fifteenth century, techniques in casting and gun making improved across western Europe and began to spread towards the countries of the Near and Middle East. Some European gun founders also travelled to these lands, taking with them their experience in artillery, including safe methods of handling the crude and volatile gunpowder. This knowledge of artillery had been perfected to create 'master gunners' and these experienced men also travelled to offer their services to rulers in these distant lands. They sought to convince them of the power of weapons, such as bombards, which the gunners could direct in the attack and defence of fortified places in return for money. The Turks had been manufacturing artillery as early as 1364, having acquired the technology through European trade routes to the west. They were quick to learn and by 1389 deployed their own field artillery at an engagement at Kosovo, where they defeated a coalition army and absorbed Serbia into their Empire.

One of the first eastern rulers to benefit from the European gun founders was Mehmet II of Turkey, 1432–81. Although only nineteen years of age, he was already an experienced soldier and it is through his imaginative use of the powerful Turkish artillery that Mehmet II, also known as 'The Conqueror', has come to be regarded as the first great gunner in history. The Turkish artillery train, which would come to terrorize their enemies, was developed largely under the guidance of European gunners. It grew to such an impressive size that by the time it was deployed at the siege of Constantinople in 1453 it included some seventy pieces. This single major action would present the world with the greatest demonstration of artillery power that had ever been seen. The weaponry in Mehmet's arsenal is known to have included nineteen particularly large guns, one of which weighed some 18 tons and was capable of firing a stone ball weighing 1,500lb (680kg) to a distance of more than a mile. On becoming Sultan in 1451, Mehmet set his ambition as being the defeat the Byzantine empire, and the crushing of the city of Constantinople for which it stood. For this purpose he gathered an army of 100,000 men around its 14 miles (22km) of perimeter walls, against which the defending garrison numbered only 7,000 men. The triple walls around

Constantinople were built around the time of Theodosius and were over 1,000 years old. They had been well maintained and had withstood an earlier attack in 1422, which led the Byzantines to depend on the strength of their defences. However, the might of the Turkish artillery train shattered the great walls in a bombardment that lasted fifty-five days.

At the start of the campaign, the Turkish artillery train was deployed in fourteen batteries containing fifty-six guns and thirteen heavy cannons in support, which could be termed 'super bombards'. Each one of these rested on a wagon formed from thirty carriages, and sixty oxen were required to move each weapon. The services of more than 200 men were needed to keep these weapons on the road and serve as guards, with a further 250 men employed just to level and repair the roads along which they were to

Mehmet II, ruler of the Ottoman Empire of Turkey between 1451–81. He was the architect of the siege of Constantinople in 1453 and the creator of the Turkish artillery force.

The Turkish Artillery Train *continued*

Artist's impression of siege of Constantinople, 1453, showing use of guns and how the gunners were dressed very lightly, as fitting their role.

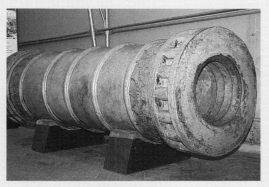

The forward or main barrel section of Mehmet's great gun. The projectile would have been loaded in here and the section screwed together. The weapon was then ready for firing.

Detail of the thread on the great gun of Mehmet as used at Constantinople in 1453. Clearly shown is the method by which capstan bars were inserted to screw the huge weapon together. This is the chamber section into which the propellant charge was loaded.

travel. Moving these guns was a slow process and it has been recorded how it took two months to move these massive weapons a distance of 320 miles (512km). These cannons could fire stone balls of almost 30in (760mm) diameter and weighing 1,100lb (500kg), but it took between two to three hours to load each piece for firing. The first massed artillery bombardment in history opened on 5 April 1453, and

nothing could have prepared the defenders of Constantinople for the power being unleashed on them.

The success of the Turkish operation has been credited as much to the power of the Ottoman artillery train as it has been to poor Byzantine preparations for the use of cannons in the defensive role. Sir Charles Oman would write much later of the action, that it was 'the first event of supreme importance whose result was determined by the power of artillery'.

The largest cannons developed huge amounts of recoil on firing, which meant that each weapon had to replaced in position after each shot. Some of the Turkish weapons were so large and took so long to load that they could fire only seven or eight rounds per day. Some estimates on the expenditure of ammunition during this great siege conservatively put the number of cannon balls fired as being in the order of some 4,000 projectiles. If this is correct, it would lead to estimate of an average of ten shots per gun for each day of fighting, which is in keeping with the length of time it took to reload each cannon.

The first breach in the outer walls was made on 18 April, but it was not wide enough to allow the Turks to make an attack. Furthermore, the guns of the Turks continued to fire at a slow rate, because if they overheated the barrels might crack. Despite the fact that the outer walls had been demolished in several places by the end of the first week of the bombardment, the

The Turkish Artillery Train *continued*

garrison still held out. The defenders and civilian population worked constantly to repair the damage, but the Turkish bombardment eventually wore them down and harrying assaults were mounted. The end came on 29 May when a particularly heavy barrage by the Turkish artillery opened a wide breach in the walls of the city. The defenders tried to halt the attackers but through sheer weight of numbers the Turkish army was victorious.

The Turks realized that it was not always practical to haul large bombards over great distances. A number of the guns in the Turkish artillery train are understood to have been built by a gun founder by the name of Urban, believed to have been working variously in Walachia or Hungary. In fact, he is thought to have cast a number of weapons directly on site at Adrianople and assisted with others, including one of a size which had never before existed. For this weapon, the Turks were obliged to transport large quantities of metal ore to the site of a siege in order to cast the weapon within their camp. They even consigned obsolete or damaged cannons to the furnace in order to melt enough metal for the huge cannon. The result was a 'terror weapon'. The massive cannon is credited to Munir Ali, who cast the weapon in two pieces, which could be screwed together for firing and

unscrewed for reloading with shot and powder in the breech end.

The writings of Kritoboulos, a chronicler (sometimes referred to as Critobulus of Imbros; the Islander), are quite revealing and he tells how the massive gun, weighing some 18 tons, as used in the siege, came to be cast. He writes how first Munir Ali gathered together a mass of the purest clay which was made malleable by many days of kneading by a host of workers. To this was added lengths of hemps and linen to strengthen it when it was formed into the mandrill for the size and shape of the weapon's bore, which tapered to one third the size at the chamber. This mandrill was then set up like a pillar and around this was moulded another layer, with a space of almost 10in between the two surfaces, to give a cylinder shape. The cylinder was then supported by a framework of timber and earth. Two furnaces were in constant use for three days and nights to melt sufficient bronze ready for casting the great barrel. The molten metal was poured into the clay mould and the mandrill was covered to an extra depth of some 35in (89cm). On cooling, the bronze contracted from the clay covering which was broken away and the barrel was ornately decorated and polished. As part of the preparation for firing the gun, it was mounted on a

Powder chamber for Mehmet's great gun. Cast in one piece at the site of the siege of Constantinople in 1453.

The Turkish Artillery Train *continued*

heavy-timbered framework which butted up to a solid wall, because the gunners believed, erroneously as it transpired, that the recoil would upset the gun's inaccurate aim. After loading a powder charge of almost 300lb (136kg) the gunners tamped in tightly-fitting wooden plugs, which could only be removed by firing the great weapon, and a stone cannon ball of about 650lb (300kg) was loaded into the barrel. On firing this mighty weapon the ball could be shot out to a range of more than 1 mile (1.6km). This weapon was called 'Elipolos', the City-taker, and it was claimed a single shot from it could destroy a tower of a castle.

In one of his works, *Life of Mohamet the Second*, which was rediscovered in the mid-nineteenth century in the Seraglio Library in the then city of Constantinople, Kritoboulos writes:

When fire is applied to the touch-hole, the powder lights quicker than thought. The discharge makes the earth around it tremble, and sends forth an incredible roar. The stone ball passes out with irresistible force and energy, strikes the wall at which it has been aimed, overthrows it, and is itself dashed into a thousand pieces.

On the defenders' side we have the written account of Jacques Tetaldi, a Florintine serving within the city, who states the Turkish forces ranged 'thousands' of heavy cannon against the city during the bombardment. But as we now know this claim was greatly exaggerated and was no doubt due to the pure terror being experienced at the time.

Another type of artillery piece which Mehmet deployed during the great siege of Constantinople was a huge mortar, which achieved at least one direct hit on a ship as it lay at anchor off the Golden Horn. Mortars were normally used to fire projectiles filled with gunpowder over short distances directly into the city at very high angles of trajectory, thus clearing the walls and exploding inside thereby causing considerable damage and injury. However, on occasion mortars had been used to engage enemy ships that had sailed too close to shore. At this time mortars were in common use across Europe and were no more than short-barrelled weapons secured to stout wooden platforms, with range adjustment being made by observing the fall of shot and varying the amount of gunpowder used to propel the projectile.

The writings of Kritoboulos, prepared in 1467, fourteen years after the great siege of Constantinople, records in some great detail how the Turks used

Overall view showing the whole of Mehmet's great 'screw' gun showing how it would have been opened for loading.

The Turkish Artillery Train *continued*

mortars in siege warfare for the first time. When Turkish ships were prevented from entering the waterway of the Golden Horn, Mehmet demanded a means of striking at the enemy's guard ships. Kritoboulos writes:

> The Emperor beholding the repulse of this attack turned his attention to the invention of another machine. He called together all those who made his guns and demanded of them if it were not possible to fire upon the ships anchored at the entrance to the port so as to sink them to the bottom. They made answer that there were no cannon capable of producing such an effect, adding that the walls of Galata hindered them on all sides ... The Emperor then proposed to them a different mode of proceeding and a totally new description of gun, of which the form should be a little modified so as to enable it to throw its shot to a great height that in falling it might strike the vessel in the middle and sink her. He explained to them in what manner, by certain proportions calculated and based on analogy, such a machine would act against shipping. And these on reflection saw the possibility of the thing, and they made a species of cannon after the outline the Emperor had made for them ... Having next considered the ground, they placed it a little below the Galata Point on a ridge which rose a little opposite the ships. Having placed it well and pointed it in the air according to the proper calculations, they applied the match and the mortar threw its stone to a great height, then falling, it missed the ships the first time and pitched very near them into the sea. Then they changed the direction of the mortar a little and threw a second stone. This, after rising to an immense height, fell with a great noise and violence and struck a vessel amidships, shattered it, sunk it to the bottom, killed some of the sailors and drowned the rest.

In July 1456, three years after the action at Constan-

tinople, the Turkish expansion had led them to besiege the city of Belgrade in Hungary. The garrison was commanded by John Hunyadi, a Transylvanian nobleman with exceptional experience of war, and under whose direction they managed to keep the Turkish forces at bay and even captured some of their artillery. In view of this, the Turks would not return until 1526. As a nation, once the Turks were intent on subduing territory it was only a question of time. In fact, as Andrew Wheatcroft states in his work *The Ottomans*:

> If the Turks lost a battle, however, they generally returned to win the war. For war was not a single campaign but a state of being until the whole of the Domain of War was embraced within the Domain of Peace. War was a season of the year, like winter and summer.

Therefore, the return of the Turks to the site of their defeats can be seen as inevitable and as a continuation of the campaign, which had never lessened even with the passing of the years.

In the east it was only the Ottomans who paid full attention to the power of artillery and continued to develop and refine their weapons over a period of time. They continued to use mercenary gunners from the west, but not all were satisfied with their position and changed sides, sometimes with dire consequences. For example a western expert, known as gunner Master George, was serving the Turkish artillery at the first siege of Rhodes in 1480. However, George deserted his Turkish masters and went over to the Christian side, where he was hanged on charges of being a spy. The Christian defenders of the island mounted such a stout resistance that the Turks were forced to abandon their operations. As with Belgrade, they were to bide their time and returned in 1522, by which time they were led by another Sultan. Under the leadership of Mehmet the Conqueror the Turks had advanced their empire on all fronts, even reaching into Italy by 1481, the year of his death. But the legacy he left meant the Ottomans would remain powerful for centuries and the power of their artillery force greatly feared.

ordered his gunners to undertake their own experiments into the relation of a gun's calibre in relation to its length of barrel. They found the optimum length was between seventeen and eighteen lengths of the bore. He ordered a number of pieces to be built to this standard, some of which were dispatched to take part in the siege of Tunis in North Africa. Twelve of these pieces were termed 'Apostles' and fired projectiles weighing 45lb (20kg). This pattern was so successful that they influenced other European designs, including Henry VIII who had his own 'Apostle' force built.

Other experiments were conducted on artillery pieces built with thinner walls to their barrels, but loaded with reduced powder charges. These trials showed that such weapons could still fire heavy projectiles, but with a significant reduction in accuracy and range. However, even the lightest of these weapons still remained clumsy and difficult to move. Some artillery pieces required a team of twenty-four horses to move them, which meant that they could not be brought into action with any great speed.

HENRY VIII'S GUN FOUNDERS

Henry VIII set about redressing the shortfallings in the English artillery forces by consolidating artisans with gun-founding skills from all over the country. Among the English gun founders to rise to prominence were the brothers Robert and John Owen, from a family of brass founders capable of casting cannons. They are believed to have begun working for the king as early as 1521 and were still casting cannons during the reign of Edward VI, Henry's son, between 1547 and 1553. Some of their pieces were even dispatched to serve in the defence of overseas English territories such the Channel Islands. One surviving piece is to be found on Jersey, where it is known to have been cast by John Owen in 1551 especially for the Parish of St Peter on the island. It is a bronze falconet, 7ft 3in (2.2m) in length with a calibre of 2.8in (70mm) and weighing some 840lb (380kg). In Jersey the artillery was stored in the Parish churches, a custom which continued until the eighteenth century.

Recreated German falconet of the late sixteenth century. Based on an original design it shows how trunnions were being cast as part of the barrel in order to allow the angle of the barrel on the carriage to be adjusted. The design also shows the handles, known as 'dolphins', which were also part of the casting and used for handling the barrel.

113

Scene from sixteenth-century manuscript depicting siege of the period. It shows how traditional weapons such as the longbow were still being used alongside gunpowder weapons, including both handguns and artillery.

Another English gun founder during Henry's reign was Ralph Hogge, who established his workshops at Buxted in Sussex, an area rich in coal deposits and iron. The Hogge foundry was producing cast iron-cannons in 1543 and continued in operation until 1614, by which time it was also producing bronze barrels.

In addition to buying cannons from Europe, Henry VIII also hired gun founders and brought them to England to cast his cannons. Their skills would be required to maintain his force and build the weapons to equip the new artillery forts which Henry would eventually order to be built at vulnerable sites along England's southern coast, such as Deal and Walmer in Kent and Pendennis and St Mawes Castles in Cornwall. He was able to contract the services of artisans such as Peter Baud (sometimes spelled Bawd) and Peter van Collen, German specialists working in France. These two men were established at the Royal Foundry and Arsenal at Greenwich in London, where they made mortars and explosive shells, with calibres up to 11in (280mm) and diameter of 19in (480mm), which John Stowe records as being:

hollow shot of cast yron stuffed with fireworks or wildfire: whereof the bigger sort of the same had screws of yron to receive a match to carry fire kin-

dled, that the fire-work might be set on fire to break in pieces the same hollow shot, whereof the smallest piece hitting any man would kill or spoil him.

Weapons known as mortars were becoming more widely used by the early sixteenth century. Their usefulness in lobbing balls and shells filled with gunpowder over the defensive walls in high arcs, where they plunged down on the target, had been recognized and they were joining the ranks of other artillery weapons.

Throughout his reign Henry continued to attract gun founders, such Franciscus Arcanus (who may also be Francesco Arcana) along with his brother Arcanus de Arcanis or Arcano, whom he recruited from Italy. There is some confusion over their names, but it is known that a gun founder with a variation on this name was in the service of Henry VIII in London from about 1529, where he was casting sakers. One of these weapons, with a length of 6ft 11in (2.1m), survives as a museum piece and was cast in Salisbury Place foundry in 1529. Such artisans not only cast cannons for the king but also instructed others in the art of gun foundry.

Producing cannons was an expensive process, and in an attempt to keep labouring costs as low as

Triple-barrelled design of cannon made during the Tudor period. Designers tried a number of such designs, but the armies preferred the traditional single-barrelled weapons, which were more reliable.

The saker was a popular weapon and the barrel for this range came in a variety of shapes and sizes. This is an English bronze saker of the sixteenth century.

Another saker with subtle differences, but it was the size of the calibre which distinguished the type of weapon. This is another English bronze cast barrel from the sixteenth century.

possible, women were sometimes employed to complete the manual work. A Bristol merchant by the name of Thomas Badock records how women were used to dig the pit into which the gun mould was placed, carry wood for the furnaces to melt the metal and dig out the barrel after casting. When cool enough they had to drag the barrel from the casting pit to a site where it was cleaned and proof fired. For their services these women were paid with cherries, bread, wine and cider. But it goes almost without saying, that men involved in gun foundry were paid wages in real money. At one point we are told that in recognition of his services, one of the Owen brothers in Henry's employ as a gun founder was paid a pension of 8 pence per day. By the same token one of the Arcanus brothers was paid a pension of 1 shilling and 4 pence per day.

IMPROVING DEFENCES AGAINST INVASION

The reign of Henry VIII was marked by a series of military campaigns, political upheavals and a break with the Roman Catholic Church, which saw England being viewed as a dangerous opponent by many European countries. One of the main points arose from the annulment of Henry's marriage to Catherine of Aragon, the aunt of Emperor Charles V, the Holy Roman Emperor, which led to a Papal Bull being issued by Pope Paul II in December 1538 and his excommunication of Henry. That in itself did not unduly worry Henry, but when the Pope united Germany and France against England as the common enemy, Henry realized the seriousness of the threat and ordered that the country take steps to prepare for war. Charles V had a very powerful and modern artillery force, with many of the field pieces having cast bronze barrels with trunnions and able to fire projectiles of cast iron. In fact, German artillery was in the ascendancy and set to become one of the most powerful forces in Europe. Thus, in early 1539 England braced itself for an invasion and put countermeasures in place. These included the construction of fortifications at

sites along England's shores which were close to the European mainland. These were built with such remarkable speed that they were completed by 1540, and included sites at Deal and Walmer in Kent and Sandown on the Isle of Wight.

These fortifications were of a new design in England and were the first true artillery forts to be built in the country. Unlike European fortifications at the time which employed ramparts and retired bastions along the design known as 'Italian Trace', Henry's new forts comprised a series of interlocked round towers which were of sexefoil design in plan view. The castles at Deal and Walmer were built partially below ground level, thereby presenting a low silhouette to attacking artillery, while at the same time providing the site with a dry moat which any attacking enemy would first have to cross. The new defences, termed Blockhouses or Bulwarks, were interlinked by a series of earthworks and were designed to protect the area of the Downs in Kent. The plans for these new fortifications have been attributed to the Bohemian engineer Stefan von Haschenberg, who may in turn have been influenced by similar designs drawn up for the defence of Antwerp by Albrecht Durer between 1520 and 1521.

Henry's new defences would eventually run along the south coast from Cornwall in the west to Dover in the east. They incorporated curved parapets to deflect cannon balls and were built in tiers to allow multiple batteries of artillery to be sited at varying heights. For example, the site at Deal is equipped with 145 embrasures for firearms and artillery can be mounted on three levels behind low parapets. These new fortifications were equipped with special vents to take away the smoke of gunpowder during firing, which would otherwise choke the gunners and hamper their vision. The construction of these new defences was in sharp contrast to those appearing in Europe at the time, but was still immensely strong. The first garrison at Deal was a force of thirty-five men commanded by Thomas Wynkfelde of Sandwich. The exact number of artillery pieces sited here is not reliably recorded, but is believed to have included demi-

The Tudor artillery fort known as Deal Castle in Kent. Built at the instigation of Henry VIII, it served to mount tiers of artillery to protect the coastal areas around strategic harbours, such as Dover.

Barrel foundry for artillery in late sixteenth century. It shows barrels being cast, including a mortar. At the top left side of the picture a worker is putting imperfect barrels back into the furnace in order to recycle the metal.

King Henry VII, father of Henry VIII. He bequeathed a rich country to his son and heir to allow the foundations of Tudor artillery to be built.

cannon firing 27lb (12kg) balls. At Calshot Castle, overlooking the Solent out towards the Isle of Wight, the complement of artillery by the end of the 1540s is recorded as being thirty-six pieces.

In the end the invasion never came, which might support the conclusion that these defences served their purpose and deterred the enemy.

EUROPEAN CAMPAIGNS

The reign of Henry VIII not only left an indelible mark on English history, it also had an influence on the history of mainland Europe. He mounted two further campaigns against France, although the first in 1523 was largely abortive. The second attack came in 1542 but he made no attempt to co-ordinate his campaign with his German allies. On the first sortie his artillery was ranged against the walls of the town of Bray in October that year. The action lasted a mere two hours between 4am and 6am when a breach 'a gap as broad as a cart' was

King Henry VIII. The founder of the English artillery train, who created many gun foundries to cast the barrels for his weapons. He also had the first artillery towers built at Deal, Walmer and St Mawes.

made in the walls. A week later at the town of Montdidier, Henry's huge siege guns moved forward until they were sited barely 40ft from the walls. Four volleys were enough to complete the work of levelling the walls, which one witness recorded as 'hard by the myghtie strong bulwerke, the strongest that evyr I saw'. Smaller pieces of artillery in the train were used in an anti-personnel role, where they wrought terrible casualties against infantry and horses which massed together in the open.

In the second of his campaigns, Henry's artillery train was ranged against Boulogne which was besieged between 19 July and 14 September

Scene depicting Tudor artillery in action during the sixteenth century. There is much activity, including loading, handling powder and shot and sighting of the weapons.

1542. In his artillery train he had ten cannons, eleven demi-cannon, twenty-one culverins, fourteen demi-culverins, thirteen falcons, twenty sakers, five bombards, one cannon-perrier, fifty mortars, fifty shrimps and seventeen small falcons. A formidable force by any standards, and although the campaign had gone well, he was forced to withdraw his forces due to lack of funds. It is no wonder, really, when it is considered how much it must have cost per day just to keep this array of weaponry in action. On top of the expenditure in gunpowder and cannon balls, there was the pay for gunners and the rest of his army.

DEVELOPMENTS IN ARTILLERY MANUFACTURE

Around this period in the sixteenth century, some gun founders were experimenting into casting cannon barrels as a solid piece, with the hollow chamber or bore being created by a new technique called reaming. Instead of being cast around a central mandrel, the new barrels were cast in one solid piece and when sufficiently cooled the clay mould was removed. The resulting casting was then taken to a site where the chamber was drilled out using a device known as a 'reamer'. This was fitted with a tool designed with three or four cutting bits on the head and varied in size according to size of the bore to be reamed. These heads could be either round or square in section, and were made from hardened metal mounted on a long rod which literally scraped out the interior of the barrel's chamber. The reamers were powered by the force of either treadmills or waterwheels, where a series of cogs and gears allowed two or three barrels to be reamed out at once. One method was to mount the barrel on a

Detail of the breech end of a sixteenth-century cannon as fitted to Henry VIII's great ship the Mary Rose. *The barrel is mounted on a wooden carriage and of a design which could also have been used on land.*

sledge-like platform, and as the head of the reamer drilled deeper into the metal, the barrel was drawn on to the tip of the borer by the gunsmiths in a controlled manner. Once the barrel was bored out the touch hole was drilled and, after finishing with hammers to flatten and smooth out the exterior surface of the barrel, it was ready for proof-firing.

Many military thinkers of the day expressed a preference for barrels made in such a manner, and they were correct in their assumption. A barrel made in such a way did not contain the fine hairline fractures often present in hollow castings, which could lead to a barrel exploding on firing. They also understood that this new method of manufacturing barrels would greatly improve the accuracy of the weapons.

Iron cannon balls were also beginning to be cast in clay moulds, which had been prepared with grease, and allowed several cannon balls to be cast in one pouring. Barrels were now being cast with trunnions and any other embellishment all before reaming, and production was greatly improved and output increased. The process of manufacturing artillery and projectiles was approaching levels of mass production.

The Need for Standardization

Gun makers and military thinkers were all the time gaining experience and starting to experiment with

Sixteenth-century cannon recreated as it would have looked at the time of being fitted to the Mary Rose. *Note the small wooden wheels on the carriage. The cannon is muzzle loaded and of a design in use on land at the same time.*

Deal Castle mounted artillery in various levels, as can be seen in this picture, and would have been a formidable weapon platform.

new designs and combinations of bore diameter and lengths of barrels. Attempts were also made to reduce the wall thickness of barrels, improve powder charges and achieve standardization of projectile weights. However, the beginning of this period of trial resulted in almost as many different types of artillery pieces as there were weapons. This led to the normal supply of ammunition becoming an almost impossible task, which in turn contributed to a partial decline in the importance of artillery in field operations.

The inconsistency in the size and categorization of artillery was a matter which could not be ignored, and a number of people applied themselves to redressing this fundamental problem. In 1544 Charles V of Germany ordered that his artillery be standardized with only seven types: cannons firing projectiles of 40lb, cannon-moyane firing projectiles of 24lb, two types of 12lb culverins, two types of 6lb culverins and a 3lb falcon.

Another to follow this trend was Henry II of France, who in 1550 ordered the establishment of six standard models for French artillery. The cannon was 10ft 6in (3.2m) length, weighing 5,200lb (2,360kg), firing a projectile of 33lb (15kg) pounds and drawn by twenty-one horses. Next was the culverin, 11ft (3.4m) length and weighing 4,000lb

(1,800kg), firing a projectile of 15lb (6.8kg) and drawn by seventeen horses. The third weapon in the range was the bastard culverin, 11ft (3.4m) length, weighing 2,500lb (1,100kg), firing a projectile of 7lb (3kg) and drawn by eleven horses. The culverin moyane was 8ft 6in (2.6m) length and weighed 1,200lb (540kg), firing a 2lb (1kg) projectile and drawn by four horses. The falcon and falconet were 7ft 6in (3.4m) and 7ft (3.2m) length respectively and weighed 700lb (310kg) and 410lb (185kg). The falcon fired a projectile of just 1lb (0.5kg) and the falconet a ball of 12oz (5.4kg) and they were pulled by three and two horses respectively.

Going even further was Prince Maurice of Orange-Nassau, who ordered that Dutch artillery be reduced to just four calibres: 6lb, 12lb, 24lb and 48lb, which could be interchanged on carriages of standardized construction.

Experimentation continued in other countries where other types of artillery were added to existing basic standard models to suit the particular needs of an army. Despite these moves, there were still no fixed standards among the weapons of different nations, and pieces of artillery fired weights of shot which gave no indication as to their size. But from now on these introductions were more restrained and entered service in a more orderly and systematic manner.

Such attempts at standardization were sometimes viewed with suspicion. In Spain, even at the end of the sixteenth century no fewer than fifty different types of cannon in some twenty various calibres were still being deployed, which must have caused severe logistical problems concerning re-supply. English artillery was little better, with sixteen different types with a range of calibres.

Naming Artillery Pieces

Along with the beginnings of standardization in calibres and sizes, certain guns were given specific names to identify them. However, although this identified the weapons it gave no clear indication of the size of projectile fired. Exactly where such names originated is unclear, though most of them appear to have been mythical birds, but the practice continued a trend which had been set in the fifteenth century. For example, one type of weapon, called the robinet, had a calibre of about 1.5in (37mm) and fired shot weighing about 1lb (0.5kg). One surviving example of a robinet, made in Austria *c.* 1570, can be seen on display in Fort Nelson,

Hampshire, England. The barrel is inscribed 'I am forsooth an uncouth peasant – who tastes my eggs won't find them pleasant', which is taken to be a reference to the ammunition. The Falcon had a calibre of some 2.5in (65mm) and fired a 3lb (1.4kg) shot. Other weapons included the saker which, depending on the country of origin, could have a calibre in the order of 3in (80mm) and fired a projectile weighing 5lb (2.3kg). The larger weapons included culverins, which could have calibres over 5in (130mm) and fired an 18lb (8.2kg) shot, and cannons, with calibres of 8in (200mm) and firing a 60lb (27kg) shot. By the end of the century methods used in gun making had reached the stage where range, power, and types of guns would hardly change over the next 300 years, or so. Most improvements made to artillery at this point mainly concerned improving its mobility, battlefield organization and tactics and field gunnery techniques.

The Elevating Screw

One of the most significant developments came in 1571, when an English gunner called John Skinner 'One of the Queen's Majesty's men', is credited

A robinet fitted with a wooden stock to create a type of giant arquebus. This would have been used from the walls of a castle to harass gunners in the besieging force.

A type of robinet which could be mounted on the walls of castles for harassing the besieging artillery crews. The robinet could be moved and sited wherever needed with relative ease and speed.

with devising the elevating screw, which was placed beneath the breech end of the barrel and gave the gunner fine control over the degree of elevation imparted to the barrel. However, one is inclined to doubt this claim because the famous engraver and military thinker, Albrecht Durer, recorded in an engraving of 1527 a cast bronze cannon of the Renaissance which is fitted with a similar device and mounted on a two-wheeled, wooden carriage. Even earlier are illustrations made by Leonardo da Vinci, who died in 1519, which showing a very basic screw mechanism to elevate the barrels of the weapons he designed. Whoever was responsible for the introduction of this device it made elevating the barrel much easier and eventually replaced the old method of hammering wooden wedges under the breach end to impart elevation which, whilst effective, could not be adjusted to the same degree as the elevating screw. However, sighting was still by direct line of vision and targets could only be fired on if they were visible to the gunners.

Ammunition

Apart from developments in the weapons, which it could be argued are actually the means of delivery,

advances were also being made into the different types of ammunition. The term 'ammunition' as applied to projectiles fired from cannons is believed to originate from this period and is understood to possibly be a corruption of the French term *munition*. The most widely used type of projectile fired from cannon was the solid cast-iron round shot.

One of the first set of trials concentrated on developing a hollow cast-iron projectile, known as a shell, which could be filled with gunpowder to burst among the enemy. Early trials were not always successful, but it was discovered that these shells were put to their best use when fired from the mortar-style weapons. The greatest difficulty was in providing an effective fuse for the shell. A basic wick-like fuse was fitted to the earliest types of shell, which was sometimes lit at the time of loading. Timing was the essential element here, because if the shell was ignited too soon it could explode before reaching the target and have no effect. If the fuse was lit too late, the shell might land and either fail to explode or, should it fall on soft ground, some of the explosive force would be absorbed. Through experimentation it was discovered that it was possible to load the shell into the barrel in such a way that when the main propelling

Artillery Pieces

Artillery of the first class consisted of long-barrelled pieces, usually about thirty calibres in length, which is to say thirty times the size of their calibre. The barrels had a thick wall to them and the pieces in this category included culverins, which were designed to fire accurately at long range.

Class I: Culverin Types 25–44 calibres in length

Type of weapon	Piece weight (lb)	Projectile weight (lb)	Bore (in)	Length (ft)	Effective range (yd)	Maximum range (yd)
Esmaril (robinet)	200	0.3	1.0	2.5	200	750
Serpentine	400	0.5	1.5	3.0	250	1,000
Falconet	500	1	2.0	3.7	280	1,500
Falcon	800	3	2.5	6.0	400	2,500
Minion	1,000	6	3.3	6.5	450	3,500
Pasavolante	3,000	6	3.3	10.0	1,000	4,500
Saker	1,600	9	4.0	6.9	500	4,000
Culverin bastard	3,000	12	4.6	8.5	600	4,000
Demi-culverin	3,400	10	4.2	8.5	850	5,000
Culverin	4,800	18	5.2	11.0	1,700	6,700
Culverin royal	7,000	32	6.5	16.0	2,000	7,000

Cast barrel of a minion. It is large and does not reflect the relatively light projectile it fired.

Bronze English falcon of the fifteenth century. Many variations were made, and it could be mounted on ships and wheeled carriages.

Recreated long-barrelled saker weapon. This had improved range and when mounted on a wheeled carriage was a useful weapon in battle, used against cavalry and infantry.

Artillery Pieces *continued*

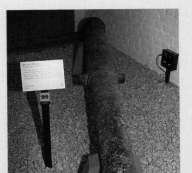

Sixteenth-century minion of Italian origin. This was a design in use across Europe, and although it fired a relatively light projectile the barrel was often quite large.

The second classification of artillery consisted of lighter, shorter pieces which were designed to fire relatively heavier projectiles but at shorter distances, thereby sacrificing range and some degree of accuracy. However, these two factors were traded off in order to achieve more mobility with little or no loss in damage-producing power when the projectile struck its target. These are the so-called cannon types of weapon, with barrel lengths of some twenty calibres.

Class II: Cannon Types 15–28 calibres in length

Type of weapon	Piece weight (lb)	Projectile weight (lb)	Bore (in)	Length (ft)	Effective range (yd)	Maximum range (yd)
Quarto-cannon	2,000	12	4.6	7	400	2,000
Demi-cannon	4,000	32	6.5	11	450	2,500
Bastard cannon	4,500	42	7.0	10	400	2,000
Cannon serpentine	6,000	42	7.0	12	500	3,000
Cannon	7,000	50	8.0	13	600	3,500
Cannon royal	8,000	60	8.5	12	750	4,000
Basilisk	12,000	90	10.0	10	750	4,000

The third and final classification of artillery consisted of shorter pieces with relatively thin walls to their barrels. These weapons were used to fire heavy projectiles for shorter ranges in the upper bracket trajectory. Included within this category were two sub-categories. Firstly, there was the pedrero, so called because it fired a stone projectile which was much lighter than an iron projectile but of the same diameter. This meant that the barrel of the pedrero could be between ten and fifteen calibres in length with quite thin walls, yet still be capable of firing a rather large stone cannon ball almost as far as a cannon. The second sub-category covered the emergent mortar. These early mortars were short, with a barrel length of ten calibres or less and fired relatively large projectiles at shorter ranges, but in a high, parabolic trajectory in order to pass over the walls of fortified towns and cities. These weapons are essentially in the same class as the type of mortars in use today.

Class III: Pedrero and Mortar Types*

Type of weapon	Piece weight (lb)	Projectile weight (lb)	Bore (in)	Length (ft)	Effective range (yd)	Maximum range (yd)
Pedrero (medium)	3,000	30	10.0	9	500	2,500
Mortar (medium)	1,500	30	6.3	2	300	750
Mortar (heavy)	10,000	200	15.0	6	1,000	2,000

* It should be noted that variations to weapons in this last group could be encountered, but pedreros were usually of ten to fifteen calibres in length and fired projectiles weighing in the order of 50lb. Some mortars could have a barrel length of only three to five calibres but still be capable of firing projectiles up to 200lb.

Detail showing mortars of the sixteenth century, which by now are fitted with elevating ratchets. This is a far cry from the basic, almost crude form, of only 100 years earlier.

charge was ignited, the flame produced would ignite the fuse of the shell. This did not eliminate the ambiguity surrounding timing, but it made handling the shell much safer. Fusing was to remain a perennial problem which would not be solved until the late eighteenth century.

Another experimental type of projectile was the canister round. This type of ammunition, dating back to at least 1410, comprised a cylinder filled with small projectiles such as lead balls or odd bits of metal, including old nails. On firing it acted like a giant modern shotgun, and was particularly lethal against infantry at very close range.

The third type of ammunition being developed for use from cannons was the grape shot, which comprised of a cluster of iron balls held in a net around a wooden tompion. This too was used against infantry and horses but at longer ranges. Although progress had been made in the types of artillery ammunition, it was still transported by wheelbarrow, horse-drawn carts or even a wicker pannier on a man's back. The artillerymen serving the cannons still walked beside their weapons and it was their pace which set the rate of progress that the field artillery made into battle.

RUSSIA

By the mid-sixteenth century the Russians were emerging as the most militaristic nation in Eastern Europe and were establishing a powerful artillery force which they termed the Pushkary. In 1502 Russian gun founders had cast a massive, single piece barrel from bronze to create a weapon called 'King of Cannons'. It was a true benchmark in barrel casting techniques for the time and was over 17ft (5m) in length. At the time it was the largest weapon of its type, at around 36in calibre (910mm) and could fire a stone ball weighing over 2,200lb (1,000kg), and was comparable to the huge guns cast for the Turkish army of Mehomet more than forty years previously. At the time of its casting, Russia was ruled by Ivan III, who had a great deal of military experience.

Under successive rulers the Russian artillery train would grow in strength and later include some very powerful weapons, one of which was called The Tsar Puschka (Great Gun of Moscow) cast in 1586. But, as the Turkish army had earlier proven, such monstrous guns had to have a practical purpose and were not cast for their aesthetic value. The effort and raw materials involved in such developments were too great to permit such an expensive move out of pure vanity.

ARTILLERY IN EUROPE

However, there then began a slight decline in the use of artillery during this century. Even so, there were very few major battles where it was not deployed in some degree, and certainly no army that valued its chances of survival in battle ever moved without its artillery train. The deployment of artillery on the battlefield was not completely ignored and it still held an important place in the order of battle. This included the attack and defence of fortifications, and artillery was also beginning to grow in the importance of naval warfare. The weapons mounted in ships were still of the types in use on land but fitted to carriages to suit naval warfare. More European armies were beginning to understand how the use of combined arms could bring them victory or halt an enemy's advance. This doctrine also extended to ships which were being deployed in fleets of ever greater numbers.

The Peasants' Rebellion in Germany

In 1525 Germany found itself torn apart by an internal uprising in the shape of a peasants' rebellion. The peasants rose in forces, sometimes numbering as many as 10,000 in one body, while other groups were as large as 25,000 and 40,000 in number. Under the leadership of Florian Geyer, a Frankish knight of lower nobility, the peasants became organized and well armed. Their weaponry included pieces of artillery hired from city states such as Rothenburg, which rented out two large artillery pieces with balls, powder and gunners. At Lake Constance peasant forces took the towns of Marktdorf and Meersdorf, which gave them thirteen pieces of artillery and 16 tons of gunpowder.

The peasants realized they could not take on the very large cities, such as Nuremburg, which was well defended with a large garrison. In open battle

they were more confident that their superior numbers could bring them victory. This was proven in July that year, when they faced a force of the Styrian nobility and captured its entire artillery train including gunpowder and ammunition. But it was not all one-sided and at Upper Allgau, the combined forces of the League of the Swabian cities and Imperial forces forced the peasants to give battle under terms that were better suited to the professional soldier. The peasant force was destroyed by concentrated artillery fire and by 1526 the rebellion disintegrated. The episode had been short-lived, but it had showed how powerful weaponry, even in the hands of peasantry, could lead to civil war and provide brief victories.

THE LOSS OF CALAIS

On 7 January 1558, after a siege lasting only several days, Calais, the last of England's territories in France, was captured by the Duc de Guise. The blame for this disaster must be shared between Mary and her dominating husband, Philip II of Spain. Mary at no time displayed any real interest in military affairs, and had allowed England to be dragged into war with France in 1556 by Philip. Calais had been abandoned to its fate when no money or troops were released for the relief of the city.

ELIZABETH I

Mary was succeeded by Elizabeth, who was the daughter of Henry VIII and of sterner stock than her half-sister. Throughout her reign as queen, Elizabeth took great interest in military matters, both on land and at sea, and showed herself to be of true Tudor stock in the same vein as her father. In fact, it was during her reign that the English finally took the step to declare the longbow obsolete from the battlefield. In a Royal Ordinance of 1595 the longbow was no longer regarded worthwhile on the battlefield, and taking this step the

Tudor warships which mounted a range of artillery, including breech- and muzzle-loaders of the same design as used by land armies across Europe.

A Tudor ship of the line. These vessels invariably carried artillery of the same type as used on land, or at least of a similar design.

A sixteenth-century cast bronze English saker. A versatile weapon, it was popular and was suitable for many roles, including mounting in ships of the line and on land.

English army became the last European army to accept firearms as official weapons for troops. By now, many of the most experienced artillerymen were reaching advanced years. For example, during the reign of Queen Elizabeth I, it is recorded how several of the gunners at the Tower of London were over 90 years old. In fact, one of the supervisors during her reign is recorded in 1580 as being Henry Pitt, who was still working at the foundry until the reign of Charles I when it was finally closed.

Queen Elizabeth's Pocket Pistol

It is interesting to note one particular piece of artillery cast in bronze by Jan Tolhuys of Utrecht in 1544. The weapon is of a type known as a basilisk which fired a 12lb (5.4kg) ball and for some reason has been nicknamed 'Queen Elizabeth's Pocket Pistol'. It was actually presented to Henry VIII by the Emperor Charles V of Germany, some fourteen years before her reign. So just how it became to be so named is something of a mystery. The weapon still survives and can be seen today at Dover Castle, Kent, where it was placed around 1613. It has a barrel length of over 24ft (7.3m) with a calibre of 5in (130mm), and believed to have a range of some 7 miles (11km). In its later history the 'Pocket Pistol' is known to have been used during the English Civil War where it formed part of the artillery train of Charles I during the siege of Hull in 1643.

On the barrel is an inscription, part of which reads:

> BREECK SCRVRET AL MEUR ENDE
> WAL BIN IC GEHETEN
> DOER BERCH EN DAL BOERT MINEN
> BAL VAN MI GESMETEN

This has been translated as follows:

> Breaker my name of rampart and wall,
> Over hill and dale I throw my ball

This has come to be regarded as a direct reference to pieces of artillery referred to as 'Wallbusters' (*Muurbraeckers*). The inscription continues 'Load me well and keep me clean, Ill carry my ball to Calais Green'. Such long-barrelled artillery pieces were popular in Germany, but in other European countries the trend in artillery was more towards smaller weapons such as Culverins, which could fire projectiles weighing in the order of 13lb (6kg), comparable to the 'Pocket Pistol'.

CAST IRON AND BRONZE CANNONS

By now cast cannon were being made from either bronze or iron and were in use with virtually all armies. The techniques of casting barrels had improved to such a point that it was obvious that this was the only way in which the barrel of a strong and practical cannon could be produced. Bronze guns had been cast in France from about 1460, but it was the strength of cast-iron guns which allowed the cast-iron cannon ball to come into common use. Bronze is produced by melting tin and copper to produce an alloy metal that has a lower melting point than iron, thereby making it easier to work. Furthermore it does not produce a large amount of air bubbles during its molten stage, a phenomenon which occurs in the process of casting and can produce a weakening of the finished weapon. Despite its cost being some ten times that of iron, a large number of artillery pieces were cast in bronze. However, cast-iron guns continued to be made in addition to these obviously superior weapons.

ARTILLERYMEN IN BATTLE

Gun positions on the battlefield were now being targeted not only by the artillery of the opposing army, but also by the cavalry who would often charge to cut down the artillerymen serving the cannons. In an effort to protect the artillery, some countries raised special units of bodyguards, later to become known as Fusilier Companies, which were detailed for the express role of protecting and guarding the artillery. However, it was not unknown for these troops to be used to prevent the gunners from running away as the enemy attacked. In most cases the overall commander of artillery was usually a soldier, but the transport and drivers were still hired in under contract and felt no obligation to remain on the battlefield if the enemy came too close. Some gunners owned their own pieces of artillery, which they hired out as mercenary forces, but even though they may have been under contract, they held no special allegiance to their masters. Their main concern was for their pieces of artillery and their lives, which would be forfeit if and when their positions became overrun by the enemy.

FORTIFYING CASTLE DEFENCES

There was also a revolution in fortification at the start of the century. High masonry walls of even the most substantial medieval fortifications were seen as vulnerable targets open to the smashing power of heavy siege guns. The garrison of such castles were often hampered in their attempts to fire back at the attackers who placed their heavy cannons beyond the range of the light guns of the defenders. Trials into mounting heavier weapons in castles were tried, but moving them around the ramparts was not easy and absorbed a great deal of manpower. On some of the older castles, it was discovered that when the cannons were fired, the recoil force threatened to destroy the walls.

In order to keep pace with developing military trends, older fortifications were massively remodelled to allow for the incorporation of artillery and provide some defence against attack by such weapons. One of the first moves was reduce the height of the walls and make them thicker, so as to make the breaching process more difficult for siege guns of the enemy, but also provide proper emplacements to site the defender's artillery. Some of the older fortifications were modernized by erecting outer walls to create bastions, with other walls being lowered and broadened where possible and covered with an earthen embankment to absorb the shock of the impact of the cannon balls. At several sites in Europe new fortifications were built along designs which incorporated broad, low walls that terminated in triangular bastions. These were known as Italian Traces from the country where they are first known to have been incorporated into modern defensive designs. They were extended to their architectural limits in order to allow the defenders to deploy their artillery to cover all possible means of approaches to the walls of the castle or fortified city. This defence was even incorporated into the fortifications on the island of Malta. In fact, it is believed that it was this feature that helped protect the island from Turkish artillery, when attacked by the forces of Suleiman II in 1565.

On other small islands, such as Jersey in the Channel Islands, castles were all but rebuilt to accommodate cannons. By 1531, the garrison of Mont Orgueil castle is recorded as having included arquebusiers (early hand-gunners), commanded by a lieutenant, with an armourer, three cannoneers, four watchmen and eighteen soldiers raised locally on the island. The cannoneers served under a Master Gunner and, along with their matrosses, fired the castle's armament which included culverins, sakers, falcons and mortars. An inventory of the castle's artillery at the time lists twenty pieces, including: 'one Fowler, one short Fowler, one three-quarter Sling, three half-Slings, two quarter-Slings, eight Serpentines, three double-Serpentines and one half-Serpentine'. The list of equipment continues with the inclusion of other 'ancillary' items connected with artillery such as '29 moulds for cannon balls, 400 lead and iron balls, 450 other sorts of cannon balls, two hammers for making stone cannon balls and various other tools'.

This was not the only site on the island to be upgraded to accept artillery. To the south of the island in the bay of St Aubin lay Fort Isabella Bellissima, as it was known at the time, sited on a rocky promontory to cover the anchorage and main settlement. Today this fortification is known as Elizabeth Castle and during the sixteenth century was re-modelled to accept artillery. The last phase came in 1590, when Sir Walter Raleigh, serving as the Governor of the island, improved the defences.

Artillery Towers

Across Europe the first real artillery towers were beginning to take shape and older Medieval fortifications were incorporated into those defences being re-modelled to accept artillery. One of the most impressive of these was Castelnaud, in the Perigord region of France. Sited on a rocky promontory which commands the surrounding Dordogne countryside, Castelnaud is known to have had artillery sited within its grounds as early as the fifteenth century. However, the first purpose-built artillery tower to be added to its structure did not come until towards the end of the sixteenth century. The structure is about 100ft (30m) in height and circular in plan view. Located at the southern end of the castle's outer defences, it has a diameter of about 45ft (14m) with the outer-facing walls having the characteristic thickening at the

Barrel of a weapon known as a serpentine. It was widely used and was often mounted on wheeled carriages in order to allow some mobility on the battlefield.

base to withstand battering by artillery fire. The tower was of very advanced design, incorporating an interior hoist through which supplies, such as gunpowder, could be transferred from one level to another. The openings, covered by trapdoors, also served to vent the smoke from artillery during battle. The tower also contains a small room between the second and third levels which has been identified as a powder magazine. It is located outside the walls of the artillery tower and abuts against the natural rock on which the castle is built. This would have greatly reduced the risk of damage to the tower should the store of gunpowder have exploded.

CHANGES IN TACTICS

In countries around Europe there was an ongoing contest between the sciences applied to improving fortifications and those used to increase the power and range of siege artillery. By using the prolonged and concentrated fire of the most powerful artillery pieces, such as the large-calibre basilisks and cannon royal, it was possible to breach the new-style defensive walls. In response to this, engineers widened the concentric ditches surrounding the fortification, which were in turn protected by counterscarp walls. These were added to by the earth excavated from the ditch, which was spread in front of them to create a sloping terrace or glacis, devoid of any cover behind which attackers might take shelter. These open slopes had deceptive gradients and added to the strength of the low walls, while at the same time further complicating the aim of the attackers who would be attempting to bring effective fire to bear on the counterscarp defenders. At designated points, the defenders could site light artillery pieces in order to keep the attackers siege artillery at a distance and spoil its accuracy. Such scientific approaches to fortification were spreading faster than the power of artillery could be developed and sieges once more were becoming campaigns of attrition.

This was not acceptable to military commanders

who now wanted a quick result in any kind of engagement. They did not want a return to the long drawn-out affairs of the past. Military engineers applied serious efforts in an attempt to prevent a return to the old ways of siege warfare, and sought to develop solutions to the problems posed by the new fortifications. They realized that the main problem facing attackers was the counterscarp and the defenders' artillery. The engineers knew that in order to defeat these it was necessary to devise a method whereby the attacking artillery and small arms could be brought close enough to the defences to bring effective fire to bear. The old methods using siege towers would be totally useless against the defenders' gunpowder weapons. They decided that the old-fashioned method of digging one's way towards the target was the best option – after all, it had been proven to work by the Turks at the siege of Constantinople in 1453.

The method they devised was to approach the enemy's position by digging a series of trenches with the engineers working under the cover of fire from long-range weapons such as culverins. The attacking engineers would simply dig a series of deep trenches, approaching the enemy's position from several points at once, until they were within range for their artillery to fire on the fortification's counterscarp. The guns would be brought forward during the night, in order to prevent them being observed by the defenders. Thick earthen walls, known as parapets, were built in front of the wide, but shallow trenches, to provide some protection to the men serving the siege guns. The defenders were aware of what was happening and could only await the final outcome while maintaining harassing fire. Once the siege artillery was in place, the attackers' would open fire on the defenders. The process was repeated until finally, under cover of artillery fire, the infantry was in a position from where it could assault forward and storm the positions of the counterscarp defenders. If the city or fortification still resisted then the attackers could move their mortars forward to fire explosive shells into the positions. This tactic was far from perfect, but it was the best that could be devised at the time.

By the end of the century this method of approaching by series of entrenchments was quite well developed and would be improved on by future military engineers.

THE POSITION OF ARTILLERYMEN

Artillerymen were by now realizing the full importance of their place on the battlefield and had started to organize themselves into guilds with master gunners, gunners and apprentices and gun-servers. It was they who understood the latent power of the gunpowder, along with the dangers involved in its handling and safe storage, every time they were deployed on the field of battle. The gunpowder had to be kept near to the cannons on the battlefield and great care had to be taken because lighted matches were present at all times, in readiness to fire the guns. It was inevitable that accidents would sometimes occur. Gunpowder could ignite without warning and when this happened the gunners were often terribly burned. For example, in 1536, Ambroise Pare, a leading medical practitioner of the time, witnessed firsthand how badly burned men were treated, following an accident with gunpowder. On entering Milan after the French attack he observed:

> Beholding them with pity there came an old soldier who asked me if there was any means of curing them. I told him no. At once he approached them and cut their throats gently and, seeing this great cruelty, I shouted at him that he was a villain. He answered me that he prayed to God that when he should be in such a state he might find someone who would do the same for him, to the end that he might not languish miserably.

Incidents such as this were common and a great deal of thought was applied into the safe transportation and storage of gunpowder. It had to be moved in carts or wagons but it was best if stored in wooden barrels, bound with rope stays, during transportation. Some countries went one stage further and provided leather liners to the barrel in order to keep the powder dry and prevent spillages. A strict set of drills governing the loading of artillery was adopted and this had a set of instructions for safe handling. One of these instructed that after each firing the barrel of the cannon had to be 'swabbed' out with water applied with either a bundle of rags or wool tied to a long-handled wooden pole. This action doused any smouldering embers which might spontaneously ignite the next charge of gunpowder as it was loaded into the barrel. Such attention to detail also applied to cannons on board ships and greatly reduced the overall number of accidents among the gunners.

REFERENCE WORKS

Books covering the theory of military subjects ranging from tactics and weaponry were beginning to be published. In this age one of the most experienced authors on the subject of artillery was Vannoccio Austino Luca Biringuccio, who had been a mine manager and metalworker from Sienna. His book *Pirotechnia* was published in 1540, two years after his death, and would be translated into several languages. The work was contained in ten volumes and covered all the known techniques of metal working of that time. In his lifetime Biringuccio had travelled across Europe learning his craft from many sources and gaining first-hand experience. He conducted advanced experiments into reducing the weight of cannons but without compromising the strength of the weapon in battle. He noted how, in his experience, there were still too many sizes for artillery pieces, but he did remark that some cannon founders were beginning to make barrels with a degree of some consistency to the thickness of the walls. Among his other observations was that some thought had been given to the problem of determining the correct calibre in relation to barrel length in order to ensure that all the powder was burnt on firing before the ball had left the muzzle of the weapon. He also expounded

Illustration showing the trajectory of a mortar projectile. Such diagrams were able to show the apprentice gunner exactly what was happening when the mortar was fired.

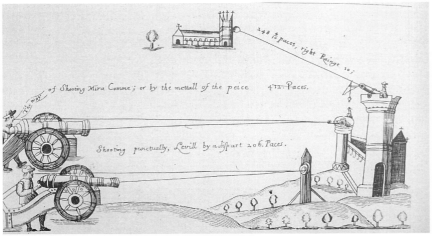

The trajectory of projectiles was just being understood and the gunner's quadrant was showing how it was important to sight the artillery properly. Here is an illustration taken from an early book on the subject, showing one of the ways in which the properties of projectiles were being interpreted.

on the advantages of iron cannonballs over stone ones, as they permitted the gunner to fire with better accuracy and greater power. However, he records that he did not regard the weapon known as the mortar with any great appreciation.

In 1586 a book entitled *The arte of shooting in great Ordnaunce* was written by William Bourne in London. It was a well-illustrated reference work and showed gunners and potential gunners how to align the bore of cannon according to the required

range, and explained how they had to know exactly where the bore lay in relation to outer lines of the muzzle and breech. Bourne's work described how this was achieved by using a rule and plumb lines and was designed to improve the accuracy of artillery.

Another author on the subject of artillery was Niccolo Tartaglia, born in Brescia, Italy in 1506. A man of peace by nature, his writings, the most famous being *Nuova Scienzia* which appeared in

1537, have led to him being regarded as the 'father of ballistics'. He was a lecturer in Verona, later becoming a professor of mathematics in Venice, while all the time writing extensively on ballistics. He formulated the theory that the greatest range of any cannon would be achieved with the barrel elevated to an angle of 45 degrees. Tartaglia is also credited with the invention of a device known as the gunner's quadrant, an 'L-shaped' instrument which was used to set the angle of elevation, and thereby give an accurate range. In use the quadrant was placed in the muzzle of the barrel, which was adjusted until the plumb line showed the correct elevation for the range required. As Tartaglia himself commented on the quadrant:

This instrument will help us to judge of all the variable positions or elevations that may happen in any peece of artillerie whatsoever ... The whole square (right angle) shall contain 144 equal parts which I call minutes.

Using his equations, gunners found that a cannonball travelled further with the barrel elevated than with the barrel at the horizontal. He joined the ranks of other authors on the subject of artillery and was also concerned with matters of fortification and:

Colloquies concerning the arte of shooting in great and small peeces of artillerie, variable

The gunner's quadrant was an essential tool and greatly improved accuracy. Some were made in very elaborate designs. The late sixteenth-century quadrant of German origin shown in these two photographs has been made in the form of an axe, in order to serve as a functional tool if required.

randges, measure and waight of leaden, yron, and marble stone pellets, mineral saltpeeter, gunpowder of divers sortes, and the cause why some sortes of gunpowder are corned and some are not corned.

OVERSEAS EXPEDITIONS

During the sixteenth century Spain and Portugal emerged as two of the foremost maritime nations, dispatching ships on great voyages of discovery. Their explorers sailed long and arduous expeditions into uncharted territories and for this reason they armed themselves with gunpowder weapons for self-protection and to quell any hostile native peoples they may encounter. Thus the use of artillery began to spread to other continents.

Cortés

One of the first expeditions was that led by Hernando Cortés, a Spanish nobleman and officer, who in 1518 landed on Hispaniola, which had been discovered by Christopher Columbus in 1492. Using the island as a secure base he sailed further west to land in Mexico, where he encountered and eventually conquered the Aztec Empire. In his force Cortés had 570 men, armed with harquebuses and ten cannons. He also had sixteen horses, animals which were hitherto unknown in the region. With his horses and gunpowder weapons, Cortés was able to bring the mighty Aztec nation to its knees. The Aztecs were armed with stone weapons and their only tactic against gunpowder weapons was to throw dust and leaves in the air. With his force increased to 850 men, fifteen cannon and eighty-six horses, by 1522 Cortés was able to establish a territory known as Nueva Espana, which is modern-day Honduras and Guatemala. This new land was rich in gold which was sent back to Spain.

Pizarro

In 1533 Francisco Pizarro, another Spanish soldier-explorer, arrived on the South American continent. He commanded a force of some 180 men, armed with harquebuses and two cannons and twenty-seven horses. With this small contingent he went on to conquer the Inca nation in modern-day Peru, all in the quest for gold. With gunpowder weapons and

The base of the breech end, known as the cascabel, showing fine detail tracery on a sixteenth-century cannon of Portuguese origin.

horses the Spanish had introduced two powerful military elements to this new continent. With horses the Spanish had exceptional mobility and their gunpowder artillery and harquebuses allowed them to kill at ranges that the natives could never envisage. At a single stroke, and using military resources that were taken for granted in Europe, the Spanish had established an empire which had almost unlimited wealth that they could harness to finance their military ventures and wars, including the Armada of 1588 which sailed against England.

Africa

The Portuguese explorers were sailing southwards towards another continent. Spain and Portugal had established trade links with North Africa, but now the explorers were sailing further and entering uncharted areas of the African coast. As with their Spanish counterparts, the Portuguese also took with them artillery and other gunpowder weapons, ostensibly for self-protection. However, not all those tribes the Portuguese encountered were amiable and the more hostile tribes were openly aggressive. These groups sought to give battle, but in a style which employed tactics completely unknown to European ideas governing warfare. The terrain and the vastnesses of this new land was alien and it was found that the massed use of gunpowder weaponry was unnecessary. Instead a simple display of force by firing several weapons was enough to deter any would be aggressor and warn them not to try and attempt such an attack. In a society which was deeply superstitious with no experience of such weapons, they were quickly and easily subdued, and the tribes were soon defeated in much the same way as the South American nations were. Through the use of gunpowder weapons two new continents had been opened and as the century progressed, artillery would open a third as Portuguese explorers pushed into the Indian sub-continent.

India

Unlike the South American and African continents, India was technically and scientifically advanced. Indeed, there is much to point towards the fact that the Indian continent may have known about the use of gunpowder weapons and artillery before the arrival of Europeans. One of the earliest engagements involving artillery was fought on 21 April 1526 at Panipat, when a Mughal force of some 10,000, commanded by Babur, clashed with a force of some 100,000 Delhi Mohammedans, led by Sultan Ibrahim, supported by 1,000 elephants. Despite being outnumbered by 10:1 it was Babur who eventually carried the battle which 'lasted till mid-day, when the enemy were completely broken and routed'.

The defeat of the Delhi Mohammedans was undoubtedly due to the fact that among Babur's forces were a number of *feringi* (foreign) cannons which he sited immediately in front of Ibrahim's war elephants. The effects as these weapons opened fire would have caused the elephants to stampede and create chaos among the enemy's ranks. Babur's victory marked the end of the Afghan dynasty of Delhi and established the Mughal Empire. Whether or not the 'foreign' cannons were supplied directly by Portuguese traders or cast in a style influenced by Portuguese gun founders is not entirely clear. But certainly as the century progressed, an increasing amount of Indian artillery was being built according to European styles.

By the time of the second Battle of Panipat, 5 November 1556, the Portuguese had been present in India for nearly sixty years. At this engagement, a Mughal army of 20,000 horsemen was led by Akbar, the grandson of Babur the first Mughal Emperor, and included a well-served artillery train. The combined forces of Hindus and rival Muslims numbered some 100,000 men and were supported by 1,500 elephants. Following on from his grandfather, Akbar's forces were able to inflict another decisive victory and reaffirm the power of the Mughal Empire.

The artillery used in India at this time was relatively old-fashioned, but still effective nevertheless. The newer barrels which replaced the ageing weapons may have been cast according to European influences, with European founders overseeing the process. Although, they were mounted on heavy carriages with four wheels which required the efforts of much manpower and draught animals to move even a small artillery train, it was possible to manoeuvre them into position, such as the siege of Rathanbhor in Rajastan in 1568, and achieve success. In barely 200 years, gunpowder weapons had been taken to all parts of the then known world and were being used to forge out empires. In other hands, artillery was also being used to end empires.

Japan

Portuguese influence extended further afield than India and reached down to the islands of Japan. The first of these expeditions landed in 1542, and with them they are known to have taken gunpowder weapons. A letter believed to describe the first sight of these weapons indicates that gunpowder may have been unknown in the outer islands of Japan:

> They carried with them one article … Which was about two or three shaku (feet) in length, straight, heavy and hollow. One end, however, was closed, and near it there was a small hole through which fire was to be lighted. The article was used in the following way – some mysterious medicine was put into it with a small piece of lead and, when one lit the medicine through the hole, the lead piece was discharged and hit everything. When it was discharged light like lightning was seen and noise like thunder was heard, so the bystanders invariably closed their ears with their hands.

The Portuguese are known to have either sold or given as gifts two weapons to Tokitaka, lord of the island, who practised with them until he could hit a target almost 'one hundred steps away'. This was obviously a musket-type match-lock firearm, but gunpowder artillery would have had exactly the same effect. Japan was to remain fiercely isolationist and as an island state could detach itself from the outside world apart from selected traders. In order to limit the spread of gunpowder weapons, strict regulations were imposed on their development in Japan. This arms regulation was to remain in place for hundreds of years, so that when the country was finally forced to open its ports to free trade in the mid-nineteenth century, traders were amazed to discover firearms being manufactured from a design which was unchanged from the sixteenth century.

Artillery at the End of the Century

By the close of the sixteenth century, gunpowder artillery had been in use for 300 years. Many changes had been made and a greater understanding of the force was obvious to many military tacticians. At various times, one country or another had risen to prominence, for example France had at one point been a leading influence but had relinquished that position to Germany. Spain had for a time also been a leading exponent of gunpowder weapons, whilst England had achieved its artillery force by using money to engage the finest gun founders from other countries. By 1600 artillery was being standardized and for at least the next 300 years artillery design would come to be influenced by five types of weapons: culverins, demi-culverins, 6lb sakers, smaller falcons and, of course, mortars and the variations of this weapon. Artillery was now firmly entrenched in military doctrine and from now on no country could afford to deploy its army without an artillery train.

Bibliography

Baumgarter, Frederick, *France in the Sixteenth Century* (Macmillan, 1985)

Bennett, Matthew, *Hutchinson Dictionary of Ancient and Medieval Warfare* (Helicon, 1998)

Bull, Stephen, *An Historical Guide to Arms and Armour* (Studio Editions, 1991)

Chandler, David, *The Art of Warfare on Land* (Hamlyn, 1974)

Cleator, P. E., *Weapons of War* (Robert Hale, 1967)

Cole, Hubert, *The Wars of the Roses* (Granada, 1973)

Comparato, Frank, *The Age of the Great Guns* (Stackpole Books, 1965)

Duffy, C., *Siege Warfare* (Routledge, 1979)

Earle, Peter, *The Life and Times of Henry V* (Weidenfeld & Nicolson, 1972)

Ffoulkes, Charles, *Arms & Armament* (Harrap, 1945)

Hewitt, John, *Ancient Armour and Weapons* (John Henry and James Parker, 1855)

Hime, H. W. L., *The Origin of Artillery* (Longman, 1915)

Hogg, Brigadier O. F. G., *English Artillery 1326–1716* (Royal Artillery Institution, 1963)

Hogg, Ian, *Fortress – A History of Military Defence* (MacDonald & Jane's, 1975)

Hogg, Ian, *The Illustrated Encyclopedia of Artillery* (Quarto, 1987)

Humble, Richard, *Warfare in the Middle Ages* (Magna Books, 1989)

Keegan, John, *A History of Warfare* (Pimlico, 1994)

Keegan, John, *The Face of Battle* (Jonathan Cape, 1988)

Koch, H. W., *History of Warfare* (Bison, 1987)

Koch, H. W., *Medieval Warfare* (Bison, 1978)

Lempriere, Raoul, *Portrait of the Channel Islands* (Robert Hale, 1970)

Macksey, Kenneth, *Guinness History of Land Warfare* (Guinness, 1973)

Montgomery of Alamein, Field Marshal Lord, *A History of Warfare* (Collins, 1968)

Needham, Joseph, *Science and Civilisation in China* (Cambridge University Press, 1956–2003)

Nicolle, David, *Medieval Warfare Source Book Volume 1: Warfare in Western Christendom* (Arms & Armour, 1995)

Nicolle, David, *Medieval Warfare Source Book Volume 2: Christian Europe and Its Neighbours* (Arms & Armour, 1996)

O'Connell, Robert, *Of Arms and Men* (Oxford University Press, 1989)

Peterson, Harold, *The Book of the Gun* (Hamlyn, 1970)

Pope, Dudley, *Guns* (Spring Books, 1969)

Reid, William, *The Lore of Arms* (Purnell Book Services, 1976)

Rogers, Colonel H. C. B., *Artillery Through the Ages* (Military Book Society, 1971)

Rybot, N. V. L., *Elizabeth Castle* (Societe Jersiaise, 1986)

Rybot, N. V. L., *Gorey Castle* (The Societe Jersiaise, 1978)

Wheatcroft, Andrew, *The Ottomans* (Viking, 1993)

Wilkinson, Frederick, *The World's Great Guns* (Hamlyn, 1977)

Index